CONTENTS

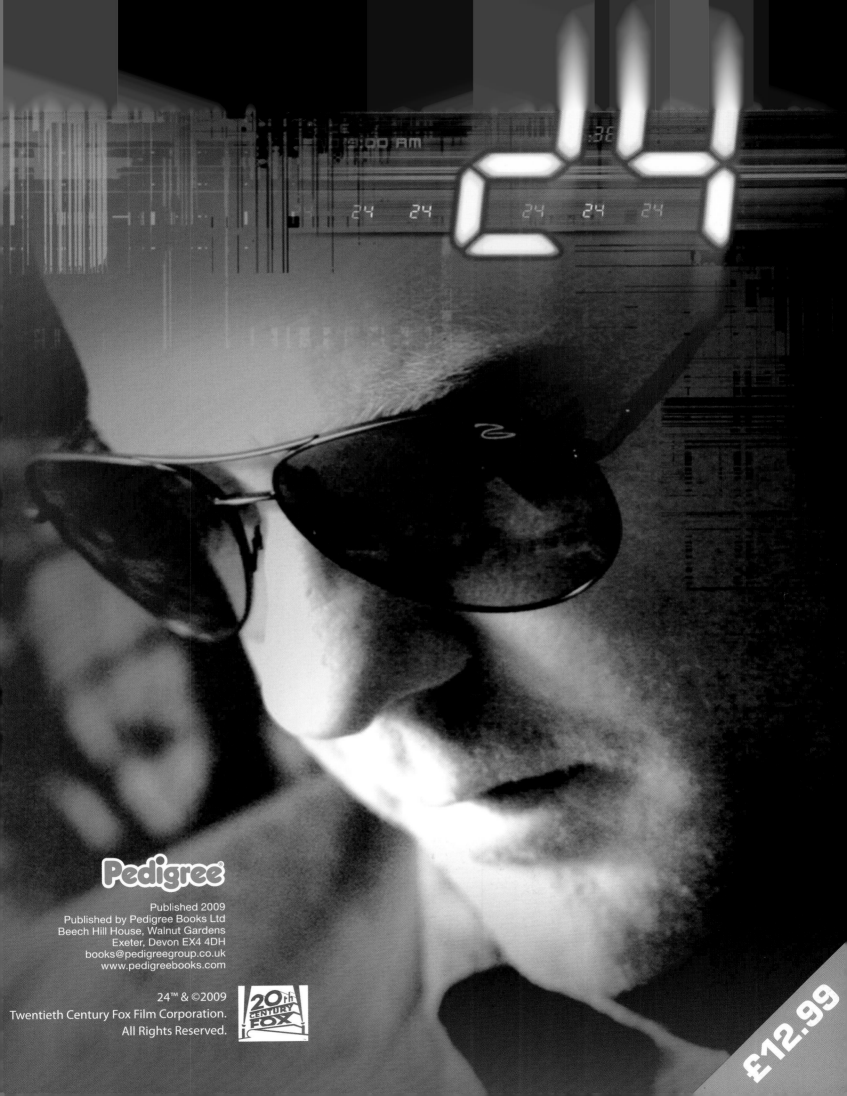

Pedigree®

Published 2009
Published by Pedigree Books Ltd
Beech Hill House, Walnut Gardens
Exeter, Devon EX4 4DH
books@pedigreegroup.co.uk
www.pedigreebooks.com

£12.99

Who hasn't heard of Jack Bauer?
He's the all-action agent who has battled to save the United States – and even the world – from nuclear attacks, war, terrorists, biological weapons and political intrigue.

Presidents have trusted him – or wanted him locked away for life! Fellow agents have had his total support – and wanted him dead!

His fight for freedom has seen him lose his wife, be separated from his love interests and even become alienated from his daughter for a period of time.

But even in his most depressed moments you can rely on Jack to fight the powers of darkness, to ward off evil and combat threats to the public.

He'll stop at nothing to achieve his goals. Jack will use the latest firepower, deadly weapons, electronic wizardry and his own cunning and intelligence to outwit his foes.

His enemies might get the better of him at times. He may have to suffer terrible pain and heartbreak but you can be sure the CTU agent will come through these adversities.

James Bond, the Mission: Impossible team, The Avengers and a whole host of other special agents and specialist espionage teams have earned a place in folklore. Jack Bauer is now among that elite!

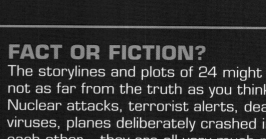

FACT OR FICTION?

The storylines and plots of 24 might not as far from the truth as you think! Nuclear attacks, terrorist alerts, deadly viruses, planes deliberately crashed into each other – they are all very much real possibilities. Some of these events have actually happened in the real world. Political intrigue, sabotage, traitors, subterfuge, conspiracies. Far fetched? Several of these things are very much real – and try to prove that some of the other incidents haven't or couldn't happen in reality. You can't!

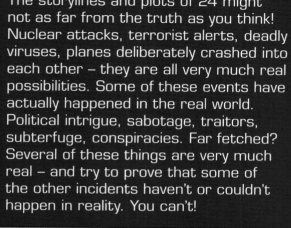

THESE ARE FOR REAL!

Generations of would-be spies and secret agents have marvelled at some of the electronic gadgets and incredible firepower handed to their heroes. Jack Bauer's tools of the trade are very much real! In a fast-developing world many of his weapons and armoury are in actual use by intelligence officers, military and police. His electronic gadgetry is also very much a part of everyday life in the 21st century. The only thing that you may not be able to get your head around is that Jack Bauer is a hero. A true legend. But then again... can you be sure he doesn't exist in real life?

CTU: COUNTER TERRORIST UNIT

BACKGROUND:

The Counter Terrorist Unit (CTU) was created following the bombing of the World Trade Centre in 1993. CTU was a domestic agency primarily responsible for maintaining homeland security and preventing terrorist attacks on the US.

CTU had its headquarters in Los Angeles, although other offices were installed in all major cities across America where threats appeared likely, such as New York and Washington. CTU was also responsible for fighting organised crime, known to fund terrorism, and involved with the creation of security policies.

CURRENT SITUATION:

Following the events of Day 6, Congress demanded that CTU be disbanded. All CTU employees had their government status revoked.

MANAGEMENT:

The head of the CTU offices is the Special Agent in Charge. The Director of Field Operations and Chief of Staff both report into the Special Agent. All of the CTU units within a region report to Divisional Office, who in turn report into District Headquarters.

Previous Special Agents in Charge have included Jack Bauer, George Mason, Tony Almeida, Erin Driscoll, Michelle Dessler, Bill Buchanan and Nadia Yassir.

The second-in-command is the Chief of Staff. They work as a deputy to the Special Agent in Charge and are generally promoted should the Special Agent in Charge be killed or removed from the role for any reason. They also run CTU when the Special Agent in Charge is unavailable.

Previous Chief of Staff include Nina Myers, Tony Almeida, Michelle Dessler and Nadia Yassir.

CTU PERSONNEL:

Most of the CTU employees are loyal to their country and dedicated to their cause. However, although personnel must pass strict security tests and entry requirements, CTU has been infiltrated by double agents and attacked by terrorist forces on several occasions. The most notable mole was Nina Myers.

ATTACKS ON CTU:

CTU has come under attack several times. Early on Day 2, bombs exploded in the CTU building, although it remained operational. During Day 3, Nina Myers activated a virus which crippled the computer systems. On Day 5, CTU was temporarily run by the Department of Homeland Security following a nerve gas attack which killed 56 CTU personnel. During Day 6, terrorists broke into CTU and workers were taken hostage.

CTU FIELD AGENTS:

CTU's field agents are required to do whatever it takes to achieve their mission. They have a wideskill-set and are expected to make quick decisions in high-pressure situations. They have extensive training with weapons and tactics.

A GUIDE TO CTU

SITUATION ROOM:
All of the most important CTU meetings take place in the situation room. It is private and secure, so it is used rather than the conference room during crisis situations. CTU is able to communicate with the President and other important people from here when necessary.

DIRECTOR'S OFFICE:
The Special Agent in Charge has an office that overlooks the Bullpen. Its elevated position allows the Special Agent in Charge to oversee everything that's going on below.

LOCATION:
The exact location of the Los Angeles branch of CTU is classified information. It is a reinforced concrete and steel building.

CONFERENCE ROOM:
Department heads use the conference room for general meetings and updates. It is equipped with monitors, phones and a large plasma screen.

INTERROGATION ROOM:
This is where suspects are quizzed by CTU officials. There is a one-way window so that suspects can be monitored during interrogation without knowing. A polygraph system and truth drugs are sometimes used to help obtain information.

MEDICAL CENTRE:
CTU's primary health care facility is fully equipped to treat both injured agents and suspects.

BULLPEN:
The open-plan hub of CTU, where personnel assess data and crisis threats. The most advanced computer technology is used. The bullpen is designed to allow for efficient communication between workers. Most of the CTU staff work in this area.

SERVER ROOM:
CTU has a large, reinforced room which houses its servers. Surveillance of any part of CTU can be done from here.

HIGHLY CONFIDENTIAL INFORMATION

JACK BAUER

DOB:
18 February, 1966

Place of Birth:
Santa Monica, California

Nationality:
US Citizen

Marital Status:
Widower (*Wife, Teri Bauer, is deceased*)

Children:
Daughter, Kimberly Bauer (*See CTU file*)

Parents:
Mother, (*unknown*)
Father, Phillip Bauer (*Deceased*)

Siblings:
Brother, Graem Bauer (*Deceased*)

Other family:
Sister-in-law, Marilyn Bauer
Nephew, Josh Bauer

Education:
- Bachelor of Arts, English Literature
  – University of California (Los Angeles)

- Master of Science, Criminology and Law
  – University of California (Berkeley)

- LASD – Basic SWAT School
- Special Forces Operations Training Course

Military Experience:
- US Army: Combat Applications Group

- US Army: First Special Forces
  Operational Detachment

- Delta Force Counter Terrorist Group

Government Experience:
- CTU: Director of Field Operations,
  Los Angeles Domestic Unit

- CTU: Former Special Agent in Charge,
  Los Angeles Domestic Unit

- CTU: Field Agent

- Department of Defense, Washington DC: Speci
  Assistant to the Secretary of Defense

- Los Angeles PD: Special Weapons and Tactic

JACK BAUER: PERSONAL PROFILE

Initially, Bauer was a highly-respected CTU field agent, who took brave and selfless action to protect his country. However, due to various events detailed in these files, Bauer has changed significantly.

Throughout his work with CTU, Bauer has made exceptional personal sacrifices for the loyalty he's shown to his country. During his time in the field he has become addicted to heroin to infiltrate the Salazar drugs ring and been held in a Chinese prison under appalling conditions. Bauer has made hundreds of dangerous enemies who would like to see him dead and also committed highly violent acts in the line of duty. He has seen all of his immediate family killed, with the exception of his daughter, Kim. The two are not close and have a troubled relationship. In fact, Bauer continually struggles to maintain any personal relationships.

These events have all affected Bauer deeply and he should be monitored closely as he is now regarded as a security risk. Bauer has repeatedly broken rules and acted outside of CTU protocol in order to achieve what he perceives to be the objective.

HK USP COMPACT

JACK BAUER: FAMILY BACKGROUND

From an early age, Bauer was expected to join his father, Phillip Bauer, working for the family business, BXJ Technologies. However, Bauer chose a different career path, and it seems Phillip never forgave him for this. The pair didn't speak for almost ten years. The role of heading the company instead went to Bauer's brother, Graem. Relations between Graem and Bauer were also sour.

Bauer has made some difficult choices regarding his immediate family, always putting loyalty to his country first. Bauer's father and brother were involved in serious threats to American homeland security. As CTU has since exposed, links were discovered between BXJ and Russian terrorists and it was BXJ who assisted the Russian terrorists obtain Sentox VX Nerve Gas, a threat dealt with during Day 5.

During Day 6, CTU unearthed evidence that suggested BXJ had been closely involved with Dimitri Gredenko, the known Russian arms dealer, and assisted him in obtaining suitcase nuclear bombs. Bauer's father took extreme action to destroy evidence that linked BXJ to the terrorist activity, including murdering Graem, his son and having his other son, Bauer, attacked. He then used his own grandson, Josh Bauer, as a hostage. As the Day 6 mission was nearing completion, Phillip attempted to kidnap Josh and flee the US for China. This resulted in Bauer shooting Phillip and leaving him to die on an oil rig. Josh was saved.

Phillip Bauer   Graem Bau

Josh Bauer   Marilyn

JACK BAUER: KEY OPERATIONS ACTIVITY SUMMARY

Day 1: Prevented assassination attempt on Senator Palmer. Wife and daughter both kidnapped. Wife killed. Bauer retired.

Day 2: At President Palmer's specific request, Bauer returned to CTU. Prevented terrorists from exploding a nuclear bomb in Los Angeles.

Day 3: Became a heroin addict to infiltrate Salazar drugs cartel. Exacted fatal revenge on Myers, the woman who killed his wife. Forced to free partner, Chase Edmunds, from Cordilla virus attached to his body by chopping off Edmunds' hand. Prevented deadly virus from being released in LA.

Day 4: Fired from CTU due to ongoing heroin addiction. Worked at the Department of Defense before returning to CTU. Prevented terrorist attacks on the US, but the mission resulted in Bauer faking his own death to avoid capture by the Chinese authorities.

Day 5: Bauer was forced out of hiding after the deaths of several close friends. Prevented a nation-wide nerve gas attack. Later captured by the Chinese authorities and held in a Chinese Military prison for 20 months.

Day 6: Bauer was returned to the US following a secret deal between President Wayne Palmer and the Chinese government. Resumed work with CTU to foil a terrorist attack, which was found to involve his father and brother, who both died. Forced to kill a fellow field agent, Curtis Manning, in the line of duty.

No further official information on Bauer's activity is available due to the disbanding of CTU following Day 6. We are aware Bauer was investigated for human rights violations after Day 6. The hearing was interrupted by news of a terrorist attack. As Bauer was assisting in averting the threat, he was exposed to fatal bio-weapon attack and his fate is unknown.

JACK BAUER'S KEY RELATIONSHIPS:

These women are considered to have had significant impact on Bauer's character:

TERI BAUER:
Jack Bauer almost sacrificed his marriage for his work with CTU. His now deceased wife, Teri, had an affair with Dr Phil Parslow and it is known that Bauer also had an affair with the disgraced CTU agent, Nina Myers, while he and Teri were separated. Teri was pregnant with Bauer's child when she was killed by Nina Myers at the age of 34. Their daughter, Kim, was 15 at the time. Since Teri's death, Bauer has struggled to form lasting relationships with women.

NINA MYERS:
During his marriage to Teri, Bauer had an affair with Myers, a fellow CTU employee. Bauer's trust in Myers was sorely misplaced. Myers was a traitor to her country and to CTU, and is now deceased. She was fatally shot by Bauer during his Day 3 mission. (*See CTU file*).

KATE WARNER:
During CTU's Day 2 mission, Bauer saved Warner from terrorists. Warner was crucial in assisting Jack and CTU defeat the terrorist plot. Warner and Bauer were involved romantically and lived together for a while, but the relationship ended between Day 2 and Day 3.

CLAUDIA HERNANDEZ:
Prior to Day 3, Bauer worked undercover within the Salazar drug cartel. Although Hernandez was the girlfriend of the cartel's leader, Hector Salazar, Bauer and Hernandez were secret lovers. Bauer attempted to free Hernandez, but during the escape effort, she was killed.

AUDREY RAINES:
It is generally believed that Raines, daughter of Secretary of Defense James Heller, was the first woman Bauer had loved since the death of his wife. Bauer eventually ended their relationship for her safety, due to the dangerous nature of his work.

HIGHLY CONFIDENTIAL INFORMATION

Career Experience:
Employed as a childminder/nanny

Government Experience:
CTU: Intern, Los Angeles, Domestic Unit

CTU: Level One Data Analyst,
Los Angeles Domestic Unit

Personal Profile:
Has worked at CTU as an intelligence agent, where she earned her place as a well-regarded employee, although she struggled at times to balance her work with concerns about her father, Jack Bauer, who was active in the field at the time. Since her mother, Teri, was murdered, Kim has had a troubled relationship with her father and they have had limited contact during previous years.

Other Information:
Kim left CTU for a new life with fellow CTU employee Chase Edmunds. Our records suggest this did not last, as she was later linked with psychiatrist Barry Landes. Kim is now married to Stephen and they have a daughter (*Further information pending*).

KIMBERLY BAUER

DOB:
(*Date and month classified*), 1987

Place of Birth:
Santa Monica, California

Marital Status:
Married, to Stephen

Children:
A daughter, Teri

Parents:
Mother, Teri Bauer (*deceased*)
Father, Jack Bauer (*See CTU file*)

Siblings:
None

Other family:
Grandfather, Phillip Bauer (*deceased*)
Uncle, Graem Bauer (*deceased*)
Aunt, Marilyn Bauer
Cousin, Josh Bauer

Education:
Santa Monica High School
(Dropped out before matriculation)

GED Certificate

Santa Monica College, Associate of Arts,
Computer Programming

HIGHLY CONFIDENTIAL INFORMATION

Key Skills:
IPSec architecture, scripts, computer vulnerabilities, intrusion detection, penetration testing, operational security, viruses, Cerberus and Plutoplus. Unit

Personal Profile:
O'Brian has proved herself to be a valuable member of the CTU team although at times her social abilities have been questioned. A skilled data analyst and programmer. Has demonstrated extreme loyalty to Jack Bauer and to other CTU employees.

Other Information:
O'Brian was deeply affected by the loss of her close colleague, Edgar Stiles, who was killed during the Sentox nerve gas attack on CTU on Day 5. O'Brian's ex-husband at the time, Morris O'Brian, was also a CTU employee. He is a talented engineer although known to be a recovering alcoholic. During the Day 5 mission, O'Brian recruited Morris to work as a freelance analyst and throughout Day 6, Morris was a critical CTU staff member. They have now re-established their relationship.

CHLOE O'BRIAN

DOB:
(*Classified*)

Place of Birth:
(*Classified*)

Marital Status:
Married to CTU employee Morris O'Brian

Children:
A son, Prescott, with her husband

Other family:
(*Classified*)

Education:
Bachelor of Science (Computer Sciences)
– University of California (Davis)

Government Experience:
CTU: Senior Analyst,
Los Angeles Domestic Unit

CTU: Intelligence Agent,
Los Angeles Domestic Unit

CTU: Internet Protocol Manager,
Los Angeles Domestic Unit

CTU: Intelligence Agent,
Washington/Baltimore Domestic

HIGHLY CONFIDENTIAL INFORMATION

Personal Profile:
Edmunds was Jack's partner and later it was revealed he had a romantic involvement with Bauer's daughter Kim. Jack was forced to amputate Edmunds' arm with an axe to remove a booby trapped virus bomb.

Other Information:
Edmunds is a bit of a hot shot having won awards for his shooting abilities, including commendations whilst with SWAT. He also won official recognition for his field work.

CHASE EDMUNDS

DOB:
May 1, 1978

Place of Birth:
California

Marital Status:
Single

Children:
Daughter, Angela, by ex-girlfriend

Education:

Washington D.C. MPD – ERT basic training

Washington D.C. MPD – Police Academy

Special Forces Operations Training Course

Government Experience:

CTU: Field Operations Agent,
Los Angeles Domestic Unit

CTU: Field Operations Agent,
Washington/Baltimore Domestic Unit

Washington D.C. MPD:
Emergency Response Team (SWAT)

HIGHLY CONFIDENTIAL INFORMATION

TONY ALMEIDA

DOB:
(*Classified*)

Place of Birth:
Chicago, Illinois

Marital Status:
Widowed at time of death
(*was married to CTU employee
Michelle Dessler, see CTU file*).

Children:
None

Other family:
(*Classified*)

Education:
- Master of Science, Computer Sciences
  – Stanford University

- Combined Bachelor of Engineering/Computer
  Sciences – San Diego State University

Career Experience:
- President of private security
  technology company

- Transmeta Corporation
  – Systems Validation Analyst

Government Experience:
- CTU: Temporary employment at Los Angeles
  Unit granted by Secretary Heller

- CTU: Special Agent in Charge, Los Angeles
  Domestic Unit.
  (*Discharged from CTU for treason, although
  was later pardoned by President Palmer*)

- CTU: Deputy Director, Los Angeles Domestic Unit

Key Skills:
Certified instructor, Krav Maga hand-to-hand
combat defense system. Excellent interrogation
techniques (example: during the Day 4 mission,
Almeida obtained important leads on Habib
Marwan's terror plans). Computer expertise,
tactical abilities. Highly respected amongst
colleagues for many years. Expert marksman.

Personal Profile:
Almeida was a steadfastly loyal agent within
CTU, and reached the position of Special
Agent in Charge. However, when his wife,
Michelle Dessler, was placed in mortal danger
during Day 3, Almeida put Dessler ahead of
the mission and was arrested for treason,
although later pardoned. Following Almeida's
release from prison, he battled with an
alcohol problem and his marriage ended,
although they later got back together. Almeida
was devastated when Dessler was killed by a
car bomb during the Day 5 mission. She was
pregnant with their first child at the time.

Other Information:
Following the events of Day 5, Almeida was
believed to be deceased for many years, but
was discovered alive during Day 7.

HIGHLY CONFIDENTIAL INFORMATION

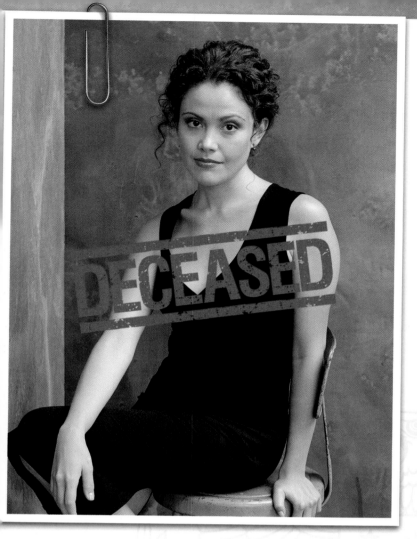

DECEASED

MICHELLE DESSLER

DOB:
(*Classified*)

Place of Birth:
(*Classified*)

Marital Status:
Married to Tony Almeida

Children:
None

Other family:
Brother, Danny Dessler

Death:
Killed by a car bomb during Day 5

Education:
- Bachelor of Science, Computer Sciences, University of Californa (Davis)

Government Experience:
- CTU: Acting Special Agent in Charge, Los Angeles Domestic Unit

- CTU: Associate Special Agent in Charge, Los Angeles Division

- CTU: Intelligence Agent, Los Angeles Domestic Unit

- CTU: Internet Protocol Manager, Los Angeles Domestic Unit

- DARPA: High Confidence Systems Working Group

- National Institute of Standards & Technology – Computer Security Division

Key Skills:
Calm under pressure and doesn't shy away from difficult decisions. Brave, loyal and a good leader.

HIGHLY CONFIDENTIAL INFORMATION

Personal Profile:
Palmer is a member of the Democratic Party. He built up a strong working relationship with Jack Bauer. Palmer did not run for re-election as President at the end of Day Three.

Other Information:
There was an assassination attempt planned on Palmer on the day of the California primary elections on Day One. He also survived an attempt to kill him with a virus, but was left confined to a wheelchair. On Day Five the former President is shot dead by a sniper and given a state procession.

DAVID PALMER

DOB:
June 2, 1954

Place of Birth:
Maryland

Marital Status:
Divorced, ex-wife Sherry

Children:
Son, Keith
Daughter, Nicole

Siblings:
Brother, Wayne Palmer

Education:
- Juris Doctor, University of Maryland School of Law
- Bachelor of Arts in Political Economy, Georgetown University

Government Experience:
- Prior to becoming he served as a Congressman and Senator.

HIGHLY CONFIDENTIAL INFORMATION

Government Experience:
CTU, Los Angeles Regional Division Director

Regional Administrator

Assistant Regional Administrator

Deputy Director of Administration, CIA

Assistant to the Deputy Director of Administration, CIA

Personal Profile:
Chappelle was a loner with few friends who associated mainly with people he worked with. He was a stickler for sticking to the rule book.

Other Information:
Chappelle reported directly to the President. He was shot dead by Jack Bauer on Day Three. The President ordered his execution after demands from terrorists.

RYAN CHAPPELLE

DOB:
1962

Place of Birth:
(*Classified*)

Marital Status:
Wife, Vicky

Children:
Son, Ryan junior
Daughters, Caitlin and Christine

Siblings:
Brother, (*Unknown*)

Education:
Master of Business Administration, Wharton

Bachelor of Science, Government, New York University

HIGHLY CONFIDENTIAL INFORMATION

NINA MYERS

Personal Information:
(*Background classified
for ongoing investigation*)

Information of Note:
Myers had a relationship with Bauer, and
was his closest confidant at CTU. She was
discovered to be a traitor during the Day
1 mission, betraying her country, CTU,
and murdering Bauer's wife, Teri. She was
incarcerated at the end of Day 1, but
negotiated a presidential pardon during
Day 2. Myers was killed by Bauer during
the events of Day 3.

HIGHLY CONFIDENTIAL INFORMATION

Government Experience:

- CTU, Programmer
- Los Angeles Domestic Unit
- Microsoft Corporation, Security Specialist
- MIT Artificial Intelligence Lab, Staff Hacker

Personal Profile:
Jamey discovered that her colleague Nina was a mole. Nina killed her and tried to make it look like suicide - but her actions were recorded on security cameras.

Other Information:
Jamey, who entered college at the age of 16, was fired from Microsoft for creating software that allowed hacking.

JAMEY FARRELL

DOB:
July 16, 1969

Place of Birth:
(*Classified*)

Marital Status:
Single

Children:
Son, Kyle

Family:
Mother, Erica Vasquez

Education:
- Bachelors of Science, Applied and Computational Mathematics - University of California
- UC Linux user group

Career Experience:
- Infosec technologies; detailed understanding of network security; proficiency in Python, Java, C/C++, Perl, LISP, HTML

HIGHLY CONFIDENTIAL INFORMATION

KATE WARNER

DOB:
February 15, 1973

Place of Birth:
(Classified}

Marital Status:
Single

Children:
None

Family:
Father, Robert
Sister, Marie

Education:
• Bachelors of Science, Economics, Stanford
  University

Experience:
• Warner International Corporation

Personal Profile:
Kate lived in Saudi Arabia for a number
of years and learnt Arabic. She had
to suffer torture at the hands of the
terrorists threatening to bomb LA as she
got dragged into the complicated plot.

Other Information:
The older of the two Warner children,
Kate was responsible for finding the
lead between her sister, Marie, and the
terrorists. This led to her having a
relationship with Jack Bauer.

HIGHLY CONFIDENTIAL INFORMATION

Personal Profile:
Mason, the second head of CTU was a mainly office-bound leader who ventured into the field, a decision which would cost him his life. He attempted to make up with his son as he was dying – and left him thousands of dollars.

Other Information:
Mason appeared as though he was trying to flee LA as terrorists got ready to explode a nuclear bomb, but in the end he was exposed to radiation. As he was dying he took over a suicide mission from Jack to crash land the bomb into the desert and save millions of people's live.

GEORGE MASON

DOB:
December 16, 1955

Place of Birth:
New York

Marital Status:
Divorced

Children:
Son, John

Education:
Bachelor of Arts, Criminal Science, University of Southern California

Government Experience:
CTU, Special Agent in Charge, Los Angeles Domestic Unit

CTU, Senior Section Leader, Washington Headquarters

CTU, Team Leader, Washington Headquarters

CTU, Associate Special Agent in Charge, Phoenix Domestic Unit

CTU, Senior Agent, Miami Domestic Unit

CTU, Agent, Los Angeles Domestic Unit

HIGHLY CONFIDENTIAL INFORMATION

WHAT DO YOU KNOW?

Amazing facts and trivia about the popular series

STAR OF THE SHOW

Kiefer Sutherland has earned a whole host of awards for his portrayal of Jack Bauer and work on 24.

The gongs include Emmys, Golden Globes and SAG Awards. He received Emmy nominations six of the show's seasons.

London-born Sutherland, who is 43 in December 2009, now spends most of his time in Los Angeles and New York.

He has appeared in more than 100 films and television series and has also worked as producer and executive producer of 24.

His parents, Donald Sutherland and Shirley Douglas, were also successful actors.

PRETTY PENNY

Penny Johnson Jerald, who plays Senator Palmer's treacherous wife, has regularly featured in other big television series.

She was in ER (nurse practitioner Lynette Evans); Deep Space Nine (freighter captain Kasidy Yates) and The Larry Sanders Show (Larry Sanders' assistant Beverly). Penny also appeared in the X-Files.

TUNED IN

MILLIONS of people all around the world watch 24 – but its success in the UK has helped it gain extra recognition in places such as Canada, Africa, Europe, Latin America, Asia, Australia, New Zealand and the Middle East.

The show has been staged mostly in Los Angeles, but Washington and New York (Series 8) have also figured. There are plans to make a big-screen version with suggestions that it could even be filmed in London.

OUT OF THIS WORLD...

Series 8 will feature Katee Sackhoff - Captain Kara "Starbuck" Thrace from the award-winning TV series Battlestar Galactica.

The Starfighter pilot plays an analyst at the New York branch of CTU and looks set to become a very popular addition to the cast.

DIRTY RAT!

The virus unleashed on the Los Angeles hotel in Series 3 is totally fictional. But it is based on a real bug known as Hantavirus pulmonary syndrome.

Hantavirus exists in North America and although it can be deadly the chances of being infected are pretty low.

The virus can be carried by rodents like rats. The first signs of infection are sickness, muscle aches and breathing problems. It can't be transmitted between humans.

There are many viruses that could be used by terrorists and this is why America set up the United States Centers for Disease Control and Prevention.

24 was the first carbon neutral television production, helping the fight against global warming.

Kiefer Sutherland, who spends ten months a year working on the programme, has actually said he would like to see Jack Bauer killed off!

The show's star man is a big fan of rock group Queen and collects guitars. He even has a model that was released by Gibson and carried his autograph.

Beroglide is a fictional drug invented by the show's writers for torture scenes. But Epinephrine does exist and is also known as adrenaline, used mostly in cardiac arrests.

24 is the second-longest running espionage series, behind Mission:Impossible and The Avengers.

Chinese television only broadcast Series One, but DVDs of all of the series are on general sale.

DAY ONE

THREAT:
Assassination plot against
Presidential candidate David Palmer

MISSION:
Can Jack Bauer rescue his
kidnapped wife and daughter?

Will he be able to protect the
Presidential candidate?

Can CTU track down the mole?

How is everything linked to
Kosovo two years earlier?

00:00–01:00

Agent Victor Rovner reports from Kuala Lumpur that a hitman is targeting Senator David Palmer, and African-American running for President.

00:05 Nina Myers, Jack Bauer's chief-of-staff at the Counter Intelligence Unit, calls him into her office. With Nina are CTU employees Jamey Farrell and Tony Almeida. High-ranking officer Richard Walsh briefs them about an expected attempt on Palmer's life. Walsh privately tells Jack there may be a leak within the CTU.

Nina confronts Jack about being excluded from a meeting with District Director George Mason. He suspects Mason skimmed money from the bust of convicted heroin dealer Phillipe Darcet. When he refused to reveal his sources Jack shoots him with a tranquiliser gun. Jack asks Nina to check Darcet's assets.

Tony, who suspects Nina is still sleeping with Jack, sends him details from the Darcet account. Jack again asks Mason who his source is and reveals the Darcet transfers. Mason relents.

00:22 On a plane bound for Los Angeles, foreign photographer Martin Belkin calls Palmer's campaign manager Patty Brooks to discuss a breakfast meeting

the next morning. Mandy, the woman sat next to him, overhears his conversation and the two strike up a rapport.

00:24 Meanwhile, Jack's daughter Kimberly and her friend Janet York have gone missing. Jack's wife Teri and Janet's father Alan go in search of the girls.

The two girls have gone to meet two guys called Dan and Rick. Kimberly asks to be driven home but Dan, who is driving, ignores her pleas.

00:45 Senator Palmer, who is writing a speech for the following day's California primary election, takes a phone call from Maureen Kingsley at the television network. He is angry at an allegation she makes.

00:52 Later Mandy goes to the back of the plane, knocks out a flight attendant, takes Belkin's stolen identification, removes a bomb from a fire extinguisher and detonates it as she parachutes to safety.

00:57 Teri and Alan York head to an address they have found on Kimberley's computer. Jack is about to join them when he hears a plane has been bombed over the Mojave Desert.

01:00-02:00

In the Mojave Desert, Mandy buries Belkin's ID card and is picked up by a car. A motorcyclist uses a tracking device to locate and dig up the card.

At a remote desert house, Mandy meets Ira Gaines who gives her a briefcase full of money. A man named Jonathan is in the house and has had plastic surgery so he looks like Belkin.

The motorcyclist, Bridgit, pulls up to the house and gives Gaines a photo of Belkin's ID before demanding extra cash.

01:09 Walsh goes to the Dunlop Plaza to secretly meet a CTU analyst named Scott Baylor. Baylor is terrified but gives Walsh a CTU key card. The magnetic strip on the card is used to access the building, but this one also contains a file on Palmer. Shots are fired. Baylor goes down and Walsh is wounded but able to call Jack for help.

Jack finds Walsh alive but as they make their escape, they kill two men. Jack, who suspects there were three, cuts a finger off one man to trace his prints.

Walsh shows Jack the key card and says to give it to Jamey who can be trusted. She will be able to reveal the dirty agent. Walsh is then killed in a hail of bullets.

Jack puts the key card into his mobile scanner and sends Jamey the information. She sends back to Jack's car mobile messenger the name of the dirty agent. It is Nina!

01:56

01:23

01:56 The missing girls aren't at the furniture store address found on the computer. When Teri can't reach Jack, she asks Nina to find the store's owner. She calls back with a phone number.

Kimberly realises Janet has been drugged. Dan orders her to call her mother on the cell phone and say she is at a party. Kimberly resists and Dan breaks Janet's arm with a crowbar. Kimberly calls her mother's cell phone and ends by telling Teri she loves her – something she never says!

01:44 Palmer's children, Keith and Nicole, return to their father's hotel suite as he gets a call from an aide named Carl who he tells about Maureen Kingsley's call. Secret Service agents warn Palmer's wife, Sherry, an attempt will be made on her husband's life.

02:02

02:27 Jack has told Teri and Alan York to remain at the furniture store for the girls. Janet is in agony with her broken arm and Rick defies Dan by giving her drugs to ease the pain.

02:32 As Rick and Dan mess about, Kim and Janet escape into an alley, where male prostitute Larry Rogow lies to cover for the girls. They bump into Rocco, a pimp who wants cash when they ask to use his mobile phone. Rogow jumps Rocco and the girls escape - but Dan and Rick spot them.
   Kim calls her mother and Teri calls 911 for help. As the girls run from Rick and Dan, a car hits Janet. The guys drag Kimberly away leaving Janet for dead.

02:39 Senator Palmer arrives at an underground garage and tells Carl of Maureen Kingsley's accusation. Several years ago, Palmer's daughter, Nicole, was raped. Kingsley claims Keith Palmer murdered the rapist. Carl agrees to find the source of the lies before the election.

02:27

02:00-03:00

Jack digitally sends the thumbprint to a CTU expert but there is no match. He returns to the Unit, hands Jamey the encrypted key card and asks her to search Nina's workstation. Jack asks Nina about the key card and the hit on Palmer but she pleads innocence.
   Jamey shows Jack and Nina a link between her computer and key card. The data was gathered on January 14th. Jack dismisses Jamey, then apologises to Nina. During that weekend he and Nina were in Santa Barbara together. Jack believes Nina's computer was hacked. She is furious he even accused her. Tony calls someone at CTU and says Jack is out of control and should be relieved of command.

02:05 Gaines orders Mandy to handle Bridgit's request for an additional million dollars for the ID card. Mandy and Bridgit argue but Bridgit appeals to Mandy's love for her, and the two kiss. Gaines agrees to the extra cash. In the desert Bridgit gives Gaines the ID but is then shot by a sniper.

02:32

36

03:00-04:00

Jack apologises to Nina for accusing her of being the leak. He says she and Jamey are the only ones he can trust.

03:10 Jamey unlocks part of the encryption on the key card and finds an address: 18166 San Fernando Road. District Director Mason arrives and issues a lockdown. Jamey hides the key card as Jack sneaks out of the office to the address.

Tony, who has discovered there was an empty seat on the blown up plane, admits to Nina he called Mason about Jack.

03:23 Mason talks to Nina about the affair she had with Jack. She tells Jamey about Mason's interrogation by Jack.

03:25 Jack finds the address where a man shoots at him and runs off. Outside, policewoman Jessie Hampton calls for backup. Jack appears and Hampton pulls her gun but after he flashes his ID they both chase the man.

Hampton is caught by the suspect, Penticoff, who tells Jack to surrender. Jack rushes him and Hampton is shot. She is taken away in an ambulance.

The suspect says he'll talk only if Jack helps him stay free. He yells to Jack: "If you ever want to see your daughter again, get me out of this!"

03:32 Kimberly is taken by Dan and Rick and gagged. As the two abductors approach Janet's body in the road, an ambulance approaches and they have to flee.

Dan and Rick meet Ira Gaines and claim they killed Janet. Gaines warns Kim she will only survive if she obeys.

Teri and Alan York are pulled over for speeding. Then a call comes over police radio confirming the 911 call about the missing girls. The pair see the ambulance that picked up Janet and head to the hospital.

03:37 Palmer returns to the hotel where his wife Sherry tells him about the assassination attempt.

He reveals Kingsley has accused their son, Keith, of murdering rapist Lyle Gibson. Gibson reportedly committed suicide. Carl has traced the allegations to Keith's therapist, George Ferragamo. Palmer now questions his son's innocence.

Agent Pierce convinces Palmer the death threat is serious and suggests calling off the breakfast meeting. Palmer refuses.

04:00-05:00

Teri and Alan York arrive at St. Mark's Hospital to find Janet in theatre. They are being questioned by a police officer in a waiting room when Jack phones. He tells Teri a man being held might have seen Kim, and says to talk to Janet as soon as she's out of surgery.

Meanwhile, Gaines orders Rick and Dan to pick up their money. The pair argue about handing over Kim. Rick is worried for Kim's welfare. Gaines pulls up to his compound, and Dan admits to not killing Janet. Gaines shoots him.

04:09 Penticoff, who is at Van Nuys police station, says he will talk only to Jack. As Mason and other agents watch from the observation room, Jack whispers to Penticoff who tells Jack to go to hell. Agents intervene as Jack attacks the suspect. Penticoff demands a call and is taken to a phone. He takes a tiny piece of paper from his mouth and dials a number. It is Jack's cell phone. Penticoff says "guys" who have Kimberly will call a phone on San Fernando Road. If Jack does not answer, it will be too late. Nina puts a trace on the phone.

04:29 At the police station, Jack approaches Phillips, Jessie Hampton's partner. He lets Jack into Penticoff's cell with his access card. There is a fight and Penticoff takes Phillips' cell access card and lets himself out.

Mason uses satellite surveillance to track Jack and Penticoff who have gone to the phone. Inside, a cell phone rings and Penticoff is told by the caller to dispose of a body in the trunk of a car. The pair find a man in the boot as Mason and other agents arrive. Jack says the body is connected to the hit on Palmer and that someone inside CTU may be involved.

Jack tells Mason that Walsh led him to Penticoff. Mason decides to interrogate Penticoff.

04:36 Palmer meets network anchor Maureen Kingsley in a private hotel conference room and asks why she is going to make allegations about Keith killing the man who raped Nicole. She has testimony from Keith's therapist, Ferragamo, and produces a document from an emergency room with the signature of Edward Johnson. The boy had wounds from a fight and the signature for Edward Johnson matches Keith's handwriting.

Palmer wakes his son, Keith, and asks him about the night after Nicole's rape. Keith refuses to answer, but says someone had to deal with it as Palmer was out of town.

05:00-06:00

Jack arrives at the CTU and hands over the body in the trunk to Nina. A helicopter whisks Jack to the hospital where he warns security to protect Janet. He then questions Alan York and tells Teri about the threat to Palmer's life. She is concerned the girls were kidnapped because of his work.

Jamey is disappointed when Nina brings in Milo, an outside contractor, to work on the key card.

Nina calls Jack to say the body has a custom-fabricated surgical pin in its ankle that can be traced to an orthopaedic surgeon. She hopes to have a name soon.

05:05 Gaines has told Rick to bury Dan at the compound. Kim tells Rick they should both try to escape since their lives are in danger. As they dig a grave Rick admits the guys were only supposed to hang out with her and Janet. Kim assures him that her father will save them.

05:05

05:05

05:37 With a threat against his campaign and family, Palmer wakes up his chief of staff, Mike Novick, and asks Carl if he knew about Keith's involvement in Gibson's death and whether he covered it up. Carl claims Keith acted in self-defence and that Sherry sent Keith to him. Novick advises Palmer to release the story at that morning's planned breakfast.

05:46 Meanwhile, Janet is awake and the doctor is optimistic about a full recovery. York is taken to see his daughter. Janet looks at him and asks who he is. York presses his hand down on her oxygen mask and suffocates her.

Jack and Teri are in the hospital hallway when Gaines, watching from the hospital security cameras, calls and tells Jack to walk away or he will kill Kimberly. Jack is led to a car in the hospital garage. Gaines briefly puts Kim on the phone.

Gaines has Jack place a small object in his ear. With this device working as a transmitter, Gaines orders Jack to throw away his cell phone and drive toward CTU.

Meanwhile, York tells Teri the girls were partying with some boys who got too aggressive. He says he has an address in Bel Air where Kim may have gone.

Teri notices a scratch on York's wrist. He received it while killing Janet, but lies about its origin. Nina calls Teri when she cannot reach Jack. Nina tells Teri to inform Jack the body in the boot is Alan York. Teri now knows the man next to her is not really York.

06:57

She had earlier overpowered Kevin and tied him up before calling the CTU where Jamey had promised to send help. Two men posing as CTU agents arrived but freed Kevin and grabbed Teri. Kim insists on staying to help her mother.

06:36 Milo soon realises all is not right and suspects Jack may have switched the cards. Nina confronts Jack with the allegation but he pulls a gun. Gaines tells Jack to take Nina from the building. He puts a jacket on Nina to hide the gun and walks to his car. Tony stops them but Jack says they are on their way to an official jurisdiction meeting. Tony asks Jamey about the meeting, but she knows nothing about it.

Nina drives as Jack gives her directions fed from Gaines through the earpiece. The car stops at an empty industrial area. Jack shoots Nina in the chest, as instructed. Men in a second car confirm to Gaines that Nina is dead.

Meanwhile, Tony scans CTU security footage and sees Jack take Nina at gunpoint. He is surprised when Nina is given a bulletproof flak jacket. At the industrial site, Nina wakes up, realises what has happened, and walks off.

06:00-07:00

Jonathon, the assassin surgically altered to look like Belkin, gets ready to leave the desert compound for the Palmer at breakfast.

06:05 Palmer asks his son to stand beside him breakfast when he makes his announcement about the Gibson murder. He refuses. His daughter Nicole is even more reluctant about reopening old wounds.

Sherry wants Palmer to blackmail Kingsley into dropping the story to save her son from prison and her husband's hopes of becoming President.

06:08 At CTU, Jack tells Nina his daughter is safe. Nina reveals the body is Alan York and he is stunned. Gaines, who has heard the conversation through the device in Jack's ear, tells Jack that Teri and Kimberly will be killed if he does not obey. Gaines instructs Jack to replace the key card given to him by Walsh with a decoy. Jack's every move is being watched on cameras set up by Gaines. He accidentally spills a drink to distract Milo so he can switch the key card.

06:31 Gaines won't let Rick leave the compound and he plans an escape. As Kim and Rick dig under a fence, Teri is dragged into the compound by Kevin, the man posing as York.

06:54

06:59

07:00-08:00

Gaines tells Jack to pick up a briefcase and sends him to Palmer's breakfast meeting at San Clarita power station.

07:08 Gaines sends Jamey an instant message and watches her on surveillance camera at CTU as she reveals Milo knows he has the wrong keycard. She is shocked to hear Nina is dead.
   Meanwhile, a dazed Nina calls Jamey's phone but gets Tony.

07:17 Tony overhears Jamey telling Milo that Nina is at an all-day meeting and that she just spoke to Nina. Tony knows she is lying. He tells Nina, who now knows Jamey can't be trusted. Nina tells Tony CTU is infiltrated.
   Jack arrives at the power plant where Secret Service Agent Pierce makes him open the briefcase, which contains a laptop computer. Jack wonders if it is a bomb.
   Jessica, Palmer's press assistant, knows Jack from high school and tries to chat. Jack moves away under Gaines's instructions. Gaines directs Jack to a closet in the plant.
   Jonathan, the assassin, arrives and takes gun parts from beneath the laptop. As the hitman puts on latex fingerprint patches, Jack is made to handle the gun.

07:32 When Nina arrives at the CTU Tony takes her to a secure room where she briefs him on Teri and Kimberly's kidnapping. They decide to warn the Secret Service about the link to Palmer.
   Tony contacts Agent Pierce and says Jack is a threat to Palmer. Nina watches as Jamey goes to the bathroom with her handheld device to pass on this information. Tony captures her. Jamey is stunned to see Nina alive and finally admits she has passed messages to an outsider.

07:54 At the Power Plant, a Secret Service agent grabs Jack and tells other agents to guard Palmer.
   Gaines orders one of his men, Eli, to kill Teri and Kim. He then notices an instant message from Jamey.
Nina and Tony, having seen the melee at the Palmer breakfast, instructed Jamey to tell Gaines that CTU ordered Jack's arrest. Gaines tells a mystery caller that a backup plan will be used and keeps the women alive.

08:00-09:00

Jack tells Secret Service Agent Simes he is protecting Palmer and warns about the assassin. He reveals how the girls were kidnapped and the plot to assassinate Palmer.

08:13 Simes sends him for questioning but Jack escapes. Still handcuffed, he grabs a gun and forces a car to stop. The driver, waitress Lauren Proctor, takes him to a construction site where Jack calls Nina to apologise for shooting her. Nina says Jamey has confessed her part in the plot. Jack instructs Nina to bring in Jamey's son, and he asks for a car and gun.

Lauren won't believe Jack's story but is forced to help him remove his handcuffs with bolt cutters. When agents arrive she gives away Jack's position but he escapes and takes their car.

08:16 Jamey, who had taken a $300,000 bribe, admits to Tony and Nina that she is working for Gaines and set up the CTU surveillance cameras. Milo is put in charge of Jamey's work and told to find out about Gaines.

Nina and Tony go to the secure room and find Jamey on the ground, bleeding from her left wrist. She has tried to take her own life. Her handheld device rings. It is Gaines calling.

08:26 Palmer and his wife Sherry return to their hotel suite. Mike Novick tells Palmer that Jack Bauer claims he was trying to protect him. Palmer recognises Jack's name, but isn't sure where from.

Sherry persuades Kingsley to hold off on the Keith story by telling her a government agent was involved in a conspiracy to kill Palmer.

08:30 At Gaines' compound, henchman Eli makes advances at Kim. Teri offers herself instead and is led away. When she returns she has a cell phone she stole from Eli. She calls Nina, but has to hang up when another thug enters the shed.

09:00-10:00

Jamey dies in hospital from her wrist wounds. Jack calls Nina from his car to ask for help in avoiding police roadblocks.

As he talks, Teri calls on the stolen mobile phone and Nina puts her through to Jack.

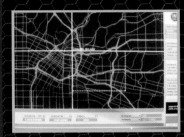

09:12 Milo tries to trace the call but can't pinpoint the spot. Teri gives clues to her location.

Police try to stop Jack but he swerves them and they chase him to a crowded parking lot. He hides under a car as Teri feeds him more information.

Eli finds the phone and takes in from Teri. He is stopped from telling Gaines by Rick who says their boss won't be happy that Teri called for help using his lost phone.

09:12

09:43

09:38 Tony finds the name Ted Cofell on Jamey's computer. Her email also shows a $1 million wire transfer to Gaines from a Swiss bank account. Cofell probably made the payment.

Jack arrives at Cofell's office and takes the driver's seat in his limo without the man noticing.

09:32 Andre Drazen calls Gaines from a Lear jet on his way to Los Angeles. He and his brother are upset the assassination has not happened. Gaines says it will before the day is over. Drazen says he will instruct Cofell to empty Gaines' bank account if the job isn't done.

09:36 Sherry calls Carl, Palmer's former aide, and asks him to prevent Kingsley from running the story. Carl admits "taking care" of evidence against Keith.

Palmer's chief of staff, Mike Novick, gets a call from Frank Ames, Palmer's biggest campaign donor. He has heard of the accusations against Keith and believes two other donors told Carl to get rid of the therapist. Ames withdraws his backing.

09:43 Alberta Green arrives at CTU as a temporary replacement for Jack. She says Jack is wanted for his part in the assassination plot against Palmer. Nina tells Green she has not heard from Jack. Green is aware of the pair's past relationship.

10:09

Carroll tells Jack that Teri and Kimberly are safe, but could die soon. Carroll agrees to take Jack to them.

10:18 Andre Drazen arrives at the desert compound, unhappy with how Gaines has handled the operation. He gives Gaines thirty minutes to find Jack before he puts his own assassination plan into operation.

He orders Gaines to get rid of Teri and Kim. Rick overhears their conversation and manages to get Dan's gun to them.

Eli enters the shed and Teri fires the gun but it is empty. Eli grabs Teri and flips open a pocketknife on Kim. Teri grabs his gun and shoots Eli dead. Teri fires a second shot to simulate the second murder and the women hide Eli's body.

10:51 Palmer arranges for Carl to meet him. Sherry says Carl took care of the evidence against Keith. Novick has discovered many gaps in Jack's background that are classified. He is surprised when Palmer asks if one gap was from summer two years earlier.

Carl arrives and claims the people who want Palmer in office will do anything to get him there. Palmer leaves a message on Ferragamo's answering machine.

10:00-11:00

Alberta Green hears Belkin filled the empty seat on the bombed plane. Nina has decided a lookalike assassin was at the political breakfast – and Green names Belkin as a suspect in the Palmer assassination attempt.

10:13 Cofell finally realises his regular driver is not at the wheel as Jack locks the doors, pulls over and draws his gun. Cofell claims not to know Gaines and says he is going to meet businessman Kevin Carroll.

Nina finds six people with that name, one the man he is due to meet. Jack drives Cofell to the meeting in an empty garage. Cofell lunges at him with a Micro Tech Halo II knife that he had hidden. Jack fights him off. Cofell curses at Jack in Serbian before dying of a heart attack.

Nina believes the hit on Palmer has a personal connection to Jack. He gets her to check Cofell's background, and research Operation Nightfall where Jack was in Belgrade and Kosovo.

The man known as Alan York gets into the car, not noticing Cofell is dead. Jack locks the doors and turns to Kevin Carroll, who has been posing as York. Carroll draws a gun and shoots at the partition – but it is bulletproof. Jack speeds off and then quickly slams on the brakes. Jack is held by his seatbelt, but Carroll slams into the partition.

10:13

10:51

DAY ONE

11:00-12:00

With Carroll tied up, Jacks takes him into the North Valley towards the compound where Teri and Kim are being held.

Nina pulls up satellite images and sees armed guards around Gaines's compound. Before she sends the photos to Jack's handheld device, she tries to persuade him to confess the truth to Alberta Green so they can send backup. He refuses, saying CTU involvement could jeopardise his family's safety.

11:11 Jack gets Carroll to drive onto the compound as he hides in the backseat with his gun pressed to the back of Carroll's head. He points to where Teri and Kim may be held, and Jack knocks him out.

Teri and Kim hide Eli's corpse and are about to leave the shed when Jack enters. He puts a chokehold on Rick but the girls beg him to let go. Rick suggests he use one of Gaines' vans to escape.

Rick is confronted by Gaines who gets a call from one of his henchmen who has found Carroll unconscious.

Green, who is convinced Nina and Tony know where Jack is, gets a call from Jack. He says he has uncovered the people behind the Palmer assassination and located their hideout.

11:42 Palmer tells his chief of staff, Novick, about Carl's plan to silence Keith's therapist. Palmer speaks to Ferragamo, but the doctor believes the Senator is threatening him and hangs up.

He wants to see Ferragamo but when they arrive at the man's office fire engines are fighting a gas explosion and he is dead. Novick and Palmer drive away.

11:54 Meanwhile, Gaines revives Carroll, who says Jack is on the premises. Gaines orders the gates to be sealed.

Guards shoot at the van carrying the Bauers, causing it to stop. A gun battle begins and Jack shoots back as he sends Teri and Kim into the woods with his handheld map. Rick stays but is clipped in the arm. Jack stabs a hole in the gas tank, and the pair depart. As Gaines and his men approach the van, Jack fires at the gas tank and the van explodes.

12:00 – 13:00

Teri and Kim head for a water tower where they are due to rendezvous with Jack and Rick. Drazen orders Gaines to deliver Jack's body. Carroll warns government agents will soon arrive. The only way for them to stay alive is to kill Jack.

12:10 Jack and Rick arrive at the tower, but Teri and Kim took another route to avoid Gaines' men. Jack calls Green who sends reinforcements. Teri and Kim find an abandoned miner's cabin but are spotted. Jack suddenly appears and shoots the man dead.

12:31 Maureen Kingsley admits she left her network job because the people trying to control Palmer had threatened her. The evidence against Keith was destroyed in the fire that killed Ferragamo.

12:44 Palmer wants to tell everything to the District Attorney but before he can Carl arrives and suggests something was planted at the Ferragamo fire that would incriminate Keith. If Palmer admits the story, Keith could be implicated in two murders. Palmer decides to maintain his run to be President.

12:51 The CTU helicopter picks up Teri and Kim. Rick has disappeared. Jack asks Gaines over a walkie talkie about the Belgrade connection and why his family was brought into this. Gaines says the people involved want to make it personal. Jack finds Gaines and is forced to shoot him dead. Wounded Rick has boarded a bus.

Nina and Tony quiz Erica Vasquez, Jamey's mother, about the cash in her bank account. Mrs. Vasquez doesn't know where the money came from. Tony and Nina discover money was transferred from a holding company based in Belgrade. Nina remembers a possible connection to Belgrade.

Green tells the news about Jack to Nina and Tony. They have discovered a wire transfer to an assassin from Belgrade. He has left Yugoslavia and is in Los Angeles.

13:00-14:00

Jack and his family arrive at CTU by helicopter. Teri and Kim are sent for a check-up at a clinic with Nina to protect them. Teri asks Dr Kent to keep her rape secret from her husband.

Nina discovers an FBI agent who says he is there to de-brief Gaines's men. A second agent has no idea about the first agent and Nina is suspicious. She calls Tony and asks for someone to dust for fingerprints. The CTU expert finds no prints – the place has been cleaned by a pro.

13:03 Nina gets permission to transfer Teri and Kim to a safe house. As they leave, the suspicious FBI agent calls someone.

Meanwhile, Green debriefs Jack who says the CIA must open their Balkan terrorist database, because Cofell had family connections there. Regional Director Ryan Chappelle interrogates Jack but wont reinstate him.

Nina calls and asks if Jack believes someone on the inside is working against Palmer. He thinks someone higher up recruited Jamey

Tony updates Green on the three shooters who may have been hired to assassinate Palmer. He only has two names.

One shooter, Alexis, has arrived from Yugoslavia and spies on Kevin Carroll. Carroll and Gaines's men are loading equipment into an abandoned house. Carroll calls Drazen and says Gaines was killed. He offers to finish the operation. Drazen says a backup plan is already in operation. Alexis blows up the house and shoots Carroll.

Chappelle tells Tony his testimony may be decisive if charges are brought against Jack. Tony says he approves of everything Jack has done since midnight.

13:45 Sherry appeals to Palmer not to reveal information about Keith or Ferragamo's death. His campaign financiers are threatening to implicate Keith in Ferragamo's murder.

Keith overhears Palmer and Novick talking about Ferragamo and Palmer has to tell his son the psychiatrist died in a fire. Keith doesn't believe the death was accidental and tells his mother he is going to the police. She stops him.

The Palmers pack their bags for a trip to an Air Force base in Nevada where they will be safe. Palmer's aide, Elizabeth Nash, leaves the hotel and says she will take a later flight after visiting an aunt. But she goes to another suite and makes love to Alexis, the hired assassin.

13:51 Mike Novick tells Palmer that Jack led a Special Forces team in Bosnia. Palmer believes Jack is seeking revenge because he lost every man on his team during that mission which was authorised by Palmer.

13:59 Palmer arrives unannounced at CTU and asks to speak to Jack Bauer.

14:53

14:22 Elizabeth Nash reveals to her lover Alexis Drazen that she has to go with Palmer to Nevada. While she showers, Alexis reads her travel itinerary.

Nash returns to the Palmer hotel suite when the campaign decides to stay in Los Angeles. She calls Alexis with the news. He briefs his brother, Andre Drazen, about the change of plans. He confirms the two other shooters have their targets in sight.

14:56 Ellis phones Jack from a bar to say the missing file was deliberately removed. As he is talking a man enters the restroom and chokes him.

Milo tells Tony the third shooter is Alexis Drazen, who stopped in Washington on his way to Los Angeles.

14:00-15:00

Chappelle orders that Palmer should not see Jack. But Palmer calls a Defense Department official who gives the ok for him to meet Jack in a secure room.

14:10 Palmer accuses Jack of wanting him dead because of the failed Operation Nightfall mission. Jack says his actions are meant to save Palmer, Teri and Kim.

Palmer reveals that Victor Drazen had been committing atrocities in Kosovo. When he was on a Senate Appropriations committee, Palmer authorised Nightfall with the object of killing Drazen. Today is the second anniversary of the mission. The assassination attempt is retaliation.

Palmer and Jack contact another operative in the mission, Robert Ellis. With Milo's help, he uncovers some data but discovers one file is missing. Milo gives Jack the report from Ellis.

Palmer and Jack read that Victor Drazen's wife and daughter were also killed in Operation Nightfall. Killing Jack's wife and daughter is direct payback. Palmer orders Chappelle to increase protection on Teri and Kim and reinstate Jack.

14:21 Hidden in the bathroom at the safe house, Teri uses a home pregnancy test that comes up positive. She confirms to Kim that it is Jack's child and it is a surprise.

Teri works out that Nina and Jack slept together whilst they were separated. Nina explains it was a mistake and Jack ended the affair.

14:18

14:22

15:00-16:00

Milo briefs Jack about the three shooters. One is Alexis, Victor Drazen's son who trained with Belgrade's special forces. Milo sends pictures of the suspected assassins to the Secret Service, and Agent Pierce shows them to Palmer's campaign team. Elizabeth Nash recognises Alexis as her lover and Jack sends a helicopter to pick her up for questioning.

Deputy Director George Mason arrives at CTU and appoints Jack as supervisor. Jack explains Palmer is a target as he chaired the sub committee that authorised the mission to kill Victor Drazen, that Robert Ellis may be dead, and that a member of Palmer's team is involved with Alexis.

Elizabeth Nash tells Mason and Jack she met Alexis in a bar. Jack wants Elizabeth to put a tracking device on Alexis when she meets him later. Although she isn't happy about seeing him again she agrees to spy for them.

15:09 Nina questions Kim about the kidnapping. Kim says Rick helped them escape but Nina believes the girl has feelings for him. Kim calls Rick and says she is covering for him. He cuts short their call when a girl named Melanie enters his room.

Outside the safe house, the dubious FBI agent from the clinic phones Andre Drazen. The man, Jovan Myovic, has killed CTU agents guarding the house. He kills another agent inside.

Inside, CTU Agent Paulson notices his fellow agents are missing and hides Teri and Kim. He faces Myovic with his gun but a second shooter named Mishko grabs him from behind. Myovic hears the women run to the garage and the shooters give chase. Paulson gets up and kills Mishko. Myovic shoots Paulson.

Teri and Kim drive off and when Teri thinks she's lost Myovic she stops the car at the side of a hill and gets out. The ground gives way and the car crashes down the cliff and explodes. A young woman named Tanya stops and gives Teri a ride. Teri can't remember her own name. Meanwhile, Kim wakes up on the side of the hill.

15:31 When Keith suggests going to the police about Ferragamo's death, Palmer says no. Keith believes his father is putting his campaign first. Keith meets Carl at the Griffith Park Observatory. Carl suggests lies could surface to incriminate Keith if he tells the truth about Ferragamo. Keith threatens to expose Carl to the moneymen behind Palmer's campaign. Keith secretly tapes their conversation.

16:39

16:00-17:00

Elizabeth Nash returns to Palmer's hotel to meet Alexis Drazen. Nina doubts Elizabeth can trap Alexis but Jack is confident. He is worried about Teri and Kim but Nina says they are safe.

Alexis informs his brother Andre that Palmer is staying in Los Angeles. Andre orders Alexis to kill Elizabeth. Jack instructs Elizabeth to place the tracking device in Alexis' wallet. He will then ring her phone so she can make an excuse to leave.

16:05 Teri is in the car with the motorist who picked her up but can't even remember being married. She recognises a restaurant and gets dropped off.

Henry, the restaurant owner, greets Teri by name and asks if Dr. Parslow will be joining her. Teri explains her memory loss, and Henry calls Dr. Phil Parslow.

16:15 Meanwhile, Kim calls CTU from a payphone and Tony answers. She says the agents at the safe house are dead but hangs up without saying where she is. Mason sends a team to the safe house.

Kim then calls Rick and is given an address in Echo Park. Rick's girlfriend, Melanie, answers the door and Kim says she wants to search Dan's room.

16:22 Keith Palmer now knows his father was protecting him from being accused of Ferragamo's murder. He plays him the tape of his conversation with Carl. Palmer takes the recording.

16:39 As Alexis pours Elizabeth a drink, she puts the transmitter inside his wallet. Jack calls her cell, but Elizabeth ignores it. Jack and Nina are shocked as Elizabeth pushes a letter opener into Alexis's stomach.

Alexis' cell phone rings. Jack answers and a man tells him to bring the money to a place called Connie's in Mid-Wilshire. He says he will be wearing a red baseball cap.

17:00–18:00

Knowing that Alexis Drazen was going to make a payoff to the intercepted caller, Jack has CTU agents search the room. They find bearer bonds, and Jack goes to California Plaza to meet with the unidentified caller.

17:11 Jack calls Tony about his family but Mason takes the phone and tells him the women are sleeping soundly. On the way to the handover, Nina tells Jack about her conversation with his wife.

Jack's backup is agent Teddy Hanlin. He had blamed Jack for arresting his ex-partner for bribes. Jack and Nina place agents around California Plaza. Hanlin is armed with a rifle.

Jack spots the man in the red baseball cap. He calls Jack "Alexis" and reveals the plan is to shut off the power grid for five minutes at 7.30pm. The man tries to flee, and against orders Hanlin shoots him.

17:11

17:36

17:53

Meanwhile, Andre Drazen calls Myovic looking for his brother, Alexis. Myovic does not know where Alexis is. Myovic goes to the Bauer home for Teri and Kimberly. Tony sends an agent to the Bauer home but Myovic kills him.

Dr. Parslow, who has told Teri he had met her when she separated from Jack, arrives at the house with Teri.

17:22 Kim realises that Rick has not told Melanie that Dan is dead.

Melanie insists Kim leave before Dan's brother, Frank, arrives. But before she can go, Frank arrives. He says Kim must stay until Dan gets there. Frank has a drug deal arranged with the money Dan and Rick were due to get from Gaines.

17:36 Palmer plays the Carl confession tape to Sherry and Novick and threatens to make it public. Novick suggests they keep it under wraps. He is certain Palmer can use it to incriminate some powerful men when he is in power.

Palmer gives an envelope to campaign manager Patty Brooks who locks it in a safe. Sherry opens the safe, sees the envelope is addressed to the District Attorney, removes the tape and destroys it. Palmer admits he had put a decoy tape in the envelope and instructs Novick to organise a press conference.

18:01

Frank's friends arrive with guns. He plans to rob the drug dealers. The dealers arrive and Frank demands the twenty thousand dollars worth of Ecstasy.

Guns are drawn and there is a standoff. The dealers drop their arms. Frank hits one dealer in the nose and he tells Frank he has the right to remain silent. He is a cop! A SWAT team bursts in arrests Frank and his friends.

18:00 At the press conference, Palmer says he misjudged some of his Los Angeles campaign backers who acted without his knowledge in murdering Ferragamo. He gives the confession tape to the authorities and says Keith will go to the police. Meanwhile, Carl watches the press conference with campaign financiers, Tuttle and Jorgensen. Palmer asks the public to back him.

18:00-19:00

Myovic watches Teri and Parslow enter the Bauer home. The doorbell rings and Parslow greets his friend, Chris, who has brought a gun to protect them.

Myovic enters the house and shoots both Chris and Parslow. He demands to know where Kimberly is. As he is about to kill Teri, Tony bursts in and shoots Myovic.

18:05 At California Plaza, Nina tells Jack the man receiving the payoff was called Alan Morgan. Palmer calls and says the retrieved missing Drazen file contains an address in California City called Saugus. The address is within the grid co-ordinates that were to be blacked out.

Mason and Jack head to Saugus, which Nina has discovered is a wildlife preserve. When Jack mentions he is happy that his family is safe, Mason become uncomfortable. Nina then hears Teri and Kimberly are missing. She asks Mason why he hasn't told Jack about his family but Mason ignores her. Mason borrows Jack's cell phone and turns it off.

As they walk through the woods, Jack tells Mason that Victor Drazen worked for Milosevic and was in charge of ethnic cleansing campaigns in Eastern Europe. They discover a new power transformer.

They keep following details from their handheld GPS as a helicopter approaches. Someone knows they are there!

18:00 Rick is forced to admit to Frank that Dan was killed. He now doesn't have the money for the drug deal and is worried.

18:28

18:40

19:00-20:00

Mason leaves for hospital after hearing that Alexis Drazen has survived surgery. Jack remains at Saugus and discovers a stairwell leading to a locked door. He is shot with a taser dart and dragged inside by security guards.

Jack awakes in a holding cell inside a secret government underground facility. Mark DeSalvo of the Department of Defense asks why Jack is there. He tells about the Palmer assassination attempt and says a power company official was bribed to cut off the electricity at 7.20pm. DeSalvo admits a prisoner is being delivered to the complex at that time.

Meanwhile, in a camouflage tent near the facility, Andre Drazen prepares his armed mercenaries.

19:19 As a helicopter approaches, Jack, DeSalvo and security men emerge from underground. Lights guide the helicopter and Drazen's men wait for the power cut. A hooded prisoner emerges from the chopper. The raid is aborted when the leading mercenary says it is too dangerous, as the lights have not gone out. Drazen decides to blow up the electrical substation for the detention facility.

19:27 Kim, Rick, Melanie and Frank are taken to the police station. Rick urges Kim to admit what has happened to her and he will accept the consequences.

Kim tells the police she knows nothing about the drug deal, gives her father's name and says she has been kidnapped. She isn't believed.

Meanwhile, at the Bauer home, Teri remembers what happened to her daughter. Tony reveals Kim is alive.

19:36 Jack finds the holding cell with the unmasked prisoner – it is Victor Drazen, the man he thought he killed two years ago in Kosovo. Victor's sons are after revenge by killing Jack's family. DeSalvo wonders why Drazen is being secretly held if the government wanted him dead. Jack says they wanted the rest of the world to believe he was dead.

Jack gets permission to interrogate the prisoner and explains to Drazen his wife and daughter were not supposed to die.

Jack asks DeSalvo to get Victor out using a way that is not on the surveillance cameras. But as they attempt to leave the lights fade and Victor warns Jack his sons have arrived.

19:46 Sherry Palmer believes her husband is giving up on the campaign but he thinks voters could side with him. He questions her about their marriage. She is confident he will never leave her, and she will be his First Lady.

20:00-21:00

Palmer wins the Super Tuesday Primary election, sweeping California and all eleven other states. Some eighty-three percent of voters back him.

20:06 Jack explains to Mason that the wildlife preserve they were in actually hides an underground detention facility where Drazen is being held. Jack begs for backup as Andre Drazen is on a rescue mission. Mason orders a field unit.

Tony brings Teri into CTU. But Nina won't reveal anything about Jack's situation. Mason tells Teri he believes Kim is safe.

Jack and DeSalvo lead Drazen down an underground hallway as an explosion blasts an entrance. They head back into the facility.

Andre Drazen's finds Jack with his gun trained on Victor. He in turn holds DeSalvo at gunpoint. As Jack releases Victor, Andre shoots DeSalvo. Victor holds Jack accountable for the fact Alexis is missing and takes him hostage.

20:29 Andre brings a cell phone with Mason on the line. He refuses to negotiate with Victor, a terrorist. To prove he is alive, Victor puts Jack on the phone. He quickly tells Mason there are six men with assault weapons.

Jack realises Victor sent a decoy into the blown up building in Kosovo and put his own family at risk. Victor admits he did not know his family would be there.

Mason finally contacts CTU Director Ryan Chappelle. Mason says Victor Drazen's escape would have embarrassed the government. Chappelle believes his release would have gone unnoticed.

Nina hears Mason order CTU troops to capture Victor Drazen even at the risk of losing Jack.

Commandos find the bodies of DeSalvo and others but not Jack or Drazen. They who may have escaped into an old sewer system, which is seeded with laser mines. They need half an hour to disarm them.

Meanwhile, Drazen's troops emerge from underground with Jack. He offers up Alexis in return for his release.

20:40 Campaign manager Patty Brooks finishes Palmer's victory speech. She is sure the country will be a better place with him in charge. Palmer memorises his speech as Patty begins to gently massage his shoulders. Palmer stops her.

20:46 Tony tells Teri that Kim has been found at a police station. Nina admits to Teri that Jack is being held prisoner.

The police car taking Kimberly to CTU is hit by a van and three masked men speaking Serbian grab her.

21:00-22:00

21:45

Jack, who is being held hostage, calls Nina at CTU and orders her to get Alexis Drazen on the line so Victor can confirm he is alive. Victor tells the CTU people listening in that he will trade Jack for Alexis.

Mason tells Nina a trade is not possible as it would be an admission that Victor is still alive and cause problems for the government.

21:15 Andre and Victor take Jack to a Slavic restaurant to hide. A man named Nikola and his daughter, Mila, welcome them. Jack grabs a knife that he holds at Mila's throat but Victor shoots Mila in the head and the guards grab Jack. Victor shoots Nikola.

Mason won't give Teri answers about the situation.

Tony hears Kimberly has been taken hostage and informs Nina.

Andre calls Mason who, having talked to Palmer, agrees to the trade. Alexis is taken to garage on Grand Avenue.

21:31 Palmer gives a speech to his supporters in the hotel banqueting room. During the speech Sherry tells Patty she wont be going to Dallas the next day and asks her to keep him company.

21:58

21:08

Palmer approaches Patty, tells her she looks beautiful and arranges to meet her upstairs in five minutes. They examine the details of Carl and the financiers' actions and Patty asks if Palmer has had any past indiscretions.

21:45 Kim is dragged into the basement and Jack sees her before a hood is placed over his head. Jack is driven to a field where there is an oilrig and tied to a post. He is told sniper rifles are aimed at him and an untraceable cell phone is placed in his pocket.

Alexis Drazen is taken in an ambulance to the garage. Mason demands Jack be handed over. A guard says they will reveal Jack's location once they have left. As their vehicle leaves Mason radios Nina who says she has it tracked.

A guard passes a signal detector over Alexis' body and finds a tracking device on the hospital wristband. He smashes it.

Meanwhile, a single shot frees Jack and via the phone in his pocket Andre tells him if he wants to see Kimberly alive he must take a nearby car and drive toward Century City.

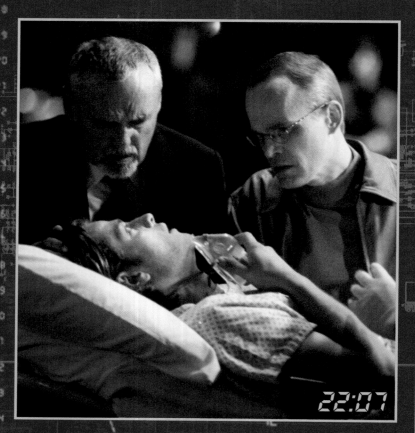

22:07

Mason realises his network access isn't working and uses. Tony's computer to check Palmer's itinerary. A new report flashes onto screens at CTU saying Palmer has been killed.

22:42 The Drazens also see the report but Victor refuses to kill Kimberly until they have confirmation Jack is dead. Andre calls the hotel and Jack offers himself for his daughter. Jack calls Nina but won't say where he is. He speaks to Teri and she reveals her pregnancy.
  Mason summons Nina and Tony and tells them Palmer is alive. Both deny speaking to Jack.
  At the warehouse, Kimberly grabs a coffeepot and throws the scalding liquid onto her guard before making a run. Kim loosens her ropes and in the dark jumps into the dock. Andre's phone rings. It is a woman named Yelena who speaks in Serbian and tells him Palmer is alive. Yelena is Nina!

22:15

22:00-23:00

Jack is instructed by Andre Drazen to head for Palmer's hotel. He wants the Senator to unfreeze $200 million of the Drazens' assets. Once that is done Jack must kill Palmer.

22:04 Palmer is alone in his hotel suite when Patty Brooks enters. Palmer hands her a key card to another room and says he will see her in 20 minutes. Patty tells Sherry about the meeting and how she feels uncomfortable.
  Sherry wants Patty to feed her information from her husband. Patty goes to Palmer who fires her for conspiring with his wife against him.
  Jack arrives having phoned Palmer. He explains Kimberly will die unless the Senator co-operates. The cell phone Jack was given rings and Palmer answers. Jack suspects a trap and throws the phone out of the window just before it explodes. Kimberly, who is being held at the Port of Los Angeles, hears the detonation from the other end of the phone. She has just seen Andre Drazen die and now fears the worst. The Drazens believe Jack and Palmer are dead.
  Sherry runs to the suite and finds her husband alive. Jack says they must pretend the Senator was killed.

22:16 Tony discovers plans of the underground detention facility have been tampered with. Nina suspects another dirty agent. When Tony learns Mason had seen the schematics, Nina orders him to shut down Mason's security access.

22:29

23:31

23:00-00:00

Kim flags down a trucker for help. He takes her to the highway patrol who call Mason and say they have a girl claiming to be Jack's daughter. Mason speaks to Kim and then orders a tactical team to the port.

23:03 Jack arrives at the docks and the cell phone rings. Andre says they know Palmer is alive and threatens to kill Kimberly. Jack calls Nina and says someone in CTU is feeding the Drazens information. Only she, Tony, Mason and Chappelle know Palmer is alive. Jack asks her to find the mole.

Nina tells Andre that Kimberly is being taken to CTU. Victor orders Nina to tell Jack that Kimberly is dead so he comes after them. Nina informs Jack that Kimberly's body was found in the water.

Jack smashes through the warehouse wall in a van, bursts out of the vehicle's back door and shoots the guards. Andre and Victor run to an approaching boat. Andre is shot dead. Victor wounds Jack in the side with his final shot. Jack moves toward Victor who tries to surrender but Jack fires round after round into his body.

23:28 Palmer makes a public statement apologising for any misunderstanding about his death. He meets with his wife and tells her he never wants to see her again, regardless of what his marriage break-up may do to his Presidential candidacy.

23:35 Jack calls Mason who confirms Kimberly is safe. Jack informs Mason that Nina is working with the Drazens. He asks for evidence.

Jack gets CTU analyst Paul Wilson to pull up security camera footage from when Jamey Farrell committed suicide. It has been erased. Jack gives Wilson access to digital backup and he uploads footage to a monitor in Jack's car. It shows Nina killed Jamey and made it look like suicide.

Mason informs his staff that Jack killed the Drazens. Elsewhere in CTU, Nina shoots a suspicious worker and then takes a laptop from a hidden safe. She calls someone and, in German, says she has been compromised. Nina spots Teri listening in and captures her.

An alarm sounds. By phone, Nina's contact orders her to go to Munich. She locks Teri in the room and leaves. Nina shoots two guards and takes a car from the garage. Jack approaches her in another car and they fire at each other.

Nina swerves into a parked car. As Jack puts a gun to her head she claims to not be working for Drazen. Mason, Tony and others approach, and convince him not to shoot her.

23:58 Jack is reunited with Kimberly but then finds Teri with bullet wounds. As Jack cradles his dead wife, he breaks down in grief and sorrow.

WEAPONS AND TECH

Your guide to great gear, amazing gizmos and electronic wizardry used by agents and villains in 24

TRANQUILISER GUN

Tranquiliser guns fire a dart carrying anaesthetic, medicine or poison and can be used to knockout or kill. These guns can only be used at short range and the darts won't penetrate protective suits or clothing. The user should aim for arms, legs, neck as fatter body sections, such as thighs, may repel the dart. The gun uses air to fire its dart and has to be recharged with a pneumatic pump action before it can fire a second shot.

OPTICAL SCANNER

Scanners are now as common as computer printers in most households. They read text or illustrations printed on paper and translate the information into a form computers can use. Jack uses a flatbed scanner in his car, which works like a photocopy machine.

HOMING DEVICE

The device used in the show to locate Martin Belkin's buried ID in Series One is fictional – but now many mobile phones have GPS technology so they can be tracked anywhere in the world. This system also allows the user to find out their location or plan routes to their destination. Even phones that do not have GPS can be tracked by using cellphone masts, which pick up their signals. GPS was launched by the US Air Force in 1993 and involved 24 satellites that orbit the earth in 12 hours. There are now often more than 24 satellites at any one time.

MICROTRANSMITTER TELEPHONES

A microtransmitter is pretty similar to the hands-free Bluetooth system you can use with your mobile phone. It's not reality yet but electronics experts are working on it! Japanese boffins have now come up with a device that is worn just like a watch, although it looks like a wristband. You talk into the band and you get a reply through the device sending vibrations from the caller's voice through your arm and to your ear canal.

MICROTECH H.A.L.O. II KNIFE

The Microtech H.A.L.O. is regarded as the standard OTF – out of the front – automatic knife. One was used against Jack by Ted Coffell on Day One. One button locks the blade safely in the closed position but it is extremely fast to open bringing its deadly four-inch blade into play.

This knife is popular with collectors and has also been used in several major films since it was first produced in 1994. There is now a H.A.LO III that has a better gripping handle, improved carry case, smooth blade without cut-outs, and a better firing button to prevent accidental blade release. Jack used this version in a later operation.

PROTECTIVE CLOTHING

Bulletproof clothing and flak jackets have been around for years and have become increasingly effective with the use of new materials.

The most significant development came in 1971 with Kevlar. This fibre is about five times stronger than steel yet weighs much less. It is one of the components used in bulletproof vests.

WIRELESS HAND HELD DEVICES

The latest generation of mobiles phones are wireless hand-held devices! They offer the lot – calls, text messaging, e-mail, internet and every other electronic device you could want. Jack Bauer eat your heart out!

DAY ONE: QUIZ

Test your knowledge of 24 with this quiz. Is your memory for detail as sharp as Jack Bauer's? Answers are on page 126.

01: What was the name of Jack Bauer's military mission in Kosovo?

(A) Operation Midnight

(B) Operation Nightfall

(C) Operation Daybreak

02: What nationality was Victor Drazen?

(A) Serbian

(B) Croatian

(C) Bosnian

03: What is the name of Kim's friend, who was kidnapped with her?

(A) Jane York

(B) Janet York

(C) Julie York

04: Who did Teri Bauer have an affair with?

(A) Dr Phil Parslow

(B) Dr Greg Flint

(C) Dr Ian Thomas

05: What is the name given to the US political primaries that take place on the same day, usually in early March?

(A) Great Friday

(B) Superb Wednesday

(C) Super Tuesday

06: Who did Kevin Carroll pretend to be in order to help Ira Gaines kidnap Teri Bauer?

(A) Alan York

(B) Adam York

(C) Adrian York

07: What kind of scandal was David Palmer's son, Keith, involved in?

(A) Underage drinking

(B) Drugs

(C) Murder

08: How many primaries did David Palmer win?

(A) 10   (B) 11   (C) 12

09: What is the name of David Palmer's daughter?

(A) Nicolette   (B) Nicola   (C) Nicole

10: Prior to his presidency, where did David Palmer serve as Congressman and Senator?

(A) Maryland

(B) Michigan

(C) Minnesota

11: What is Jack Bauer's masters degree in?

(A) Psychology and Criminology

(B) Criminology and Law

(C) Law and Psychology

12: Who was hired by the Drazens to assassinate Senator David Palmer?

(A) Kevin Carroll

(B) Ira Gaines

(C) Greg Penticoff

DAY TWO

TIMELINE:
18 months after Day One

THREAT:
A nuclear bomb is due to explode in Los Angeles.

MISSION:

Can Jack track down the terrorist bombers?

Who are the real masterminds behind the bomb?

Will the conspirators overthrow the President?

Can all-out World War be prevented?

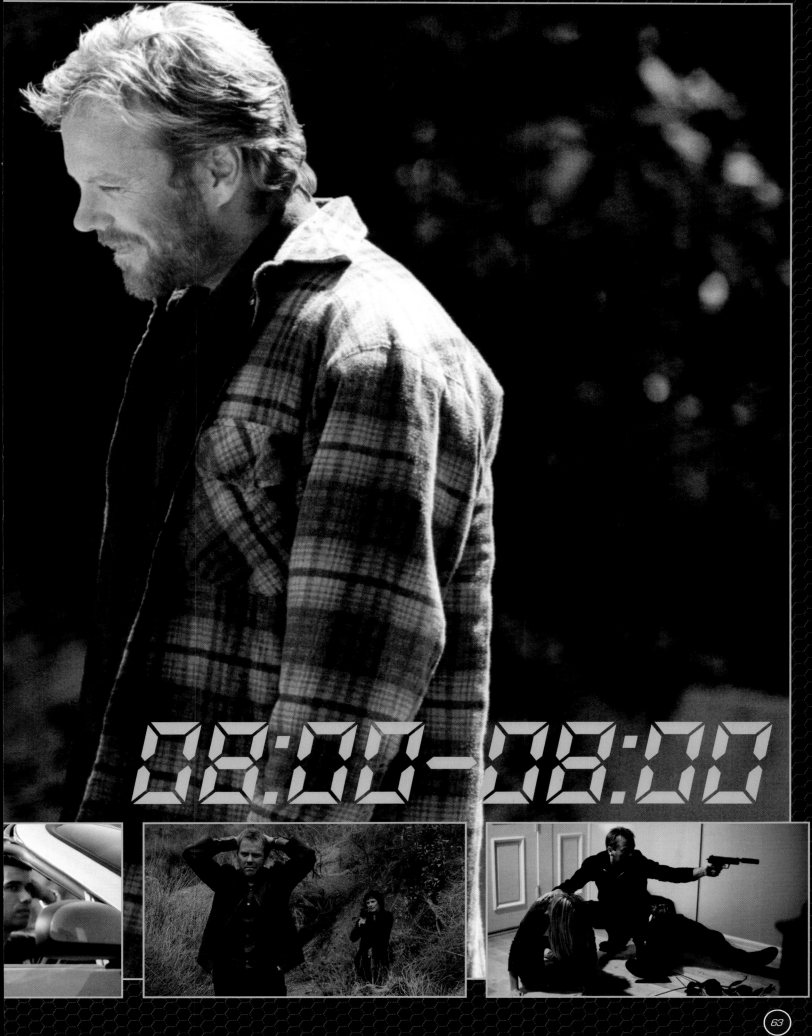

08:00-09:00

08:31

08:00-09:00

In Seoul, Korean Jason Park is being tortured for information. He says the word "today" to American military officers who immediately contact Eric Rayburn at the National Security Agency.

President Palmer and his son Keith are fishing from a boat on Lake Oswego in Oregon when their Secret Service agent relays a message.

Palmer is shuttled to the North West Regional Operations Complex to meet Rayburn and District Director George Mason. Rayburn tells the President and chief aide, Lynne Kresge, that terrorists have placed a nuclear device in Los Angeles, and it is set to go off today.

Agents tracking Park spotted him with suicide bomber Mamud Rashed Faheen, who they thought had been killed in a West Bank bombing. Faheen is controlled by a splinter group called Second Wave, and one Middle Eastern state is unofficially affiliated with them.

08:08 Palmer speaks to that country's Prime Minister who denies any link to Second Wave. Palmer says he is aware of an attack and threatens retaliation.

Mason informs CTU staff about the nuclear bomb and orders total secrecy. Tony Almeida and Mason believe inactive agent Jack Bauer has a connection to the case.

Rayburn tells the President that if the bomb explodes there could be two million casualties. The President refuses military action.

New CTU programmer Paula Schaeffer admits to Tony that she may not be able to work under such stressful conditions.

08:16 Unshaven and unkempt, Jack Bauer returns to his townhouse, after an aborted attempt make up with his daughter Kim. She is working as a nanny to nine-year-old Megan Matheson and can't let him back into her life after the death of her mother.

Jack ignores messages from CTU on his answering machine. The phone rings again and when Jack hears President Palmer's voice he picks up. Palmer wants his help.

Mason tells Jack about the bomb and says he is needed to help identify a prime suspect. Jack calls Kimberly and tells her to leave Los Angeles. But she hangs up. Jack says he will track down the bomb as long as two specific agents pick up Kim.

Mason reveals that a Joseph Wald has been connected to Second Wave. Jack had previously worked undercover and arrested Wald, who is currently missing. Jack says to bring in Marshall Goren, the key witness against Wald in a trial.

Michelle creates a fake criminal background for Jack. Mason instructs the FBI to send Goren to CTU for questioning. He refuses to talk as the Feds have already promised a deal. Jack shoots Goren in the chest and asks Mason for a hacksaw!

08:18 A man of Middle Eastern decent named Reza Naiyeer drives up to the Warner estate in San Fernando Valley. He greets his fiancé, Marie Warner, with a kiss. She is making final preparations for their wedding. Her sister, Kate, and her father, Bob, are helping.

Kate takes a phone call from Ralph Burton, a private investigator she hired to check on Reza's finances. He has discovered Reza had dealings with an international terrorist named Syed Ali.

Meanwhile, a man named Marko arrives at a building in an industrial park and speaks to a man at the door in Arabic. Inside, armed guards surround an area that has radiation symbols. People working with gloved hands pour a coloured powder into a container. Marko hears the bomb will be ready soon.

08:59 Kimberly Bauer is in her room with Megan, when the youngster's father Gary Matheson pulls up to the house. They hear Gary yell at Carla and Kim locks the door. Gary claims Carla has had an accident and warns Kim if she says anything he will hurt her.

08:49

09:00-10:00

Michelle briefs Jack about Wald's crew, and Jack recognises one photo as Eddie Grant, who he befriended while undercover.

Jack is told that when Agent Grothy went to pick up Kim, she had gone. He calls his daughter's cell phone, not knowing she has left it in the Matheson house. Kim has stolen their car to take Megan away from her violent father. He leaves a message warning her to leave Los Angeles.

Mason hears forged Middle Eastern passports have been found in a car and match those of the suspects. He sends his closest agent, which is Grothy.

09:09 Jack goes into a salvage garage and asks for Wald. He is met by Grant, who knows him as Jack Roush. Eddie accuses Jack of putting Joe in jail, but Jack says he has news about Goren turning state's evidence to convict Joe. Jack gives Eddie his bag, and Goren's head rolls out. Eddie smiles.

Eddie takes Jack to see Dave. Jack claims he just served five years for Joe, and wants to see him. Dave checks Jack's record online as Paula traces his actions on her computer. As no cover information is loaded, Paula fills something in quickly.

Dave is working with explosive. Jack secretly calls Mason and then watches as duffel bags are put into a van.

Jack tells Eddie that Dave is an amateur as he tied the fuses too tight. They fight and Dave's ankle is broken. Jack is asked to replace Dave on the job – to bring down the CTU offices in Los Angeles!

09:16 Palmer gives an informal press briefing and jokes about his trip being cut short. But press secretary Jenny Dodge says a reporter named Ron Wieland suspects something is wrong.

Wieland claims he has heard the Alert Condition has changed due to a threat and will go live with the story at noon. Palmer agrees a private interview with Wieland and asks for Jenny to contact Richard Armus. Palmer tells the reporter his information is wrong. He agrees to think about sitting on the story.

As he leaves, Wieland is stopped by Armus, who introduces himself as part of the President's Secret Service team, then leads him away.

Kim drives Megan to a police station but is trapped in an alley by Gary's car and a truck. Kim and Megan run and hide.

09:40 Megan complains that her head hurts from when her dad pushed her. She promises to hide whilst Kim makes a 911 call. Gary surprises her before she can dial but she hits him with a tyre iron and he falls down.

10:00–11:00

Eddie won't tell Jack why CTU is being targeted. Kim calls Jack and asks for help. He tells her to go to her Aunt Carol's house in San Jose. But she doesn't understand why as she hasn't heard his earlier messages.

CTU phones are corrupted as Eddie's crew takes out lines at the relay station. Jack calls the O.C. and asks for the President. Lynne takes the call. Lynne and Rayburn presume the CTU attack is a diversion from the nuclear bomb. Rayburn stops her telling CTU as he believes this will blow Jack's cover.

Rayburn has had CTU transfer their intelligence, so the only losses would be infrastructure and personnel. Palmer is not happy and orders Lynne to notify CTU immediately.

10:11 Two telephone repair workers arrive at the relay station. Eddie shoots one and orders the other to call his boss to say he must go to CTU and check the phones. At CTU, the worker gets past security with Eddie and his men in the back of his van.

With the others gone, Jack releases the phone worker, explaining he is undercover. He gives him a note for Tony that warns there are bombs in CTU. Jack cuts

struck on the head and knocked out. As the team return and pull away in the van, Kim and Megan arrive.

Michelle gives Tony the note from the telephone worker and he orders an immediate evacuation. Kim and Megan are escorted out as Tony runs up to Mason's office to save Paula, who is still trying to complete the data transfer. They are caught inside the building when it explodes.

10:21 As Mason heads out of Los Angeles on a job, he is redirected to Panorama City where police have found a vehicle linked to someone on the terrorist watch list. Police find the area where Marko's team were building the weapon. There is a shoot-out with hidden gunmen that sends a powder into the air. Mason notices radiation warning signs. He coughs as he calls for a Hazmat team.

Mason calls Tony and says he will send fingerprints from the dead bodies. He is told about CTU's database being transferred and says the same request should have been made to other agencies.

A Hazmat doctor informs Mason he has inhaled a high level of enriched plutonium and may only have one day to live.

10:30 At the Warner house, Kate gets a call from private investigator Ralph Burton. He confirms Reza has had contact with the terrorist. Burton must tell

11:00-12:00

11:30

Eddie takes a call from Wald and scribbles down his address. Jack pulls his gun on Eddie and demands the note. The rest of the crew shoot at Jack who kills them before shooting Eddie.

Jack arrives at the address in Simi Valley and tells Joe that Eddie and the crew are dead. Joe opens the door and Jack takes him at gunpoint. Joe is surprised when Jack says the CTU explosion was a diversion for a nuclear bomb. He will not admit who ordered the CTU bomb.

A pit bull leaps at Jack and Joe escapes into a nearby shed. Jack shoots the dog and follows. Joe is locked in a room with steel doors and Jack pleads to him, saying more than a million innocent people could die.

The door opens and Joe hands Jack an envelope with photos of his female contact before shooting himself in the mouth. The woman in the photos is Nina Myers.

11:03 Palmer is visibly upset over the bombing. Lynne blames Rayburn for the casualties but he says she was the one who spoke to Jack and has to take the blame.

Later, Palmer and his advisors watch a news report about the bombing. Rayburn again asks about evacuation. Palmer has reservations.

Palmer tells Lynne he knows about the thirty-minute lapse between Jack calling and CTU being informed. Lynne offers her resignation but Palmer refuses it.

The President fires Rayburn, who he knows held back on the warning. Rayburn insists he acted so Jack could get to Wald. Agents take Rayburn to Richard Armus.

Mason is told he should be ok for another twelve hours but then his mental functions will deteriorate and he go into a coma.

11:34 Kim, who is unaware that Gary Matheson has told the police she kidnapped his daughter, carries Megan out of the rubble at CTU. Suddenly the youngster's eyes roll back and she begins to seize. A Paramedic takes her to hospital where a doctor says the problem was caused by a skull fracture before the CTU explosion. She has other prior injuries that indicate physical abuse.

Kim phones Carla, Megan's mother, and tells her about the abuse. Carla is stopped from going to hospital by her husband Gary.

11:45 Tony, who escaped from the bombing, reports on the casualties. Paula, who had encrypted all intelligence about the nuclear threat, was seriously injured.

When he returns to CTU, Mason asks for Paula to be woken, even though he is told she will die without hospital treatment.

At the Warner house, Kate tells her father there are inconsistencies in their company's budget and that she hired a private investigator to discover if Reza had been stealing. Kate has learned Reza may be involved with a terrorist. Bob Warner doesn't believe her. He had Reza checked himself.

Kate goes to collect lunch and Bob insists her future brother-in-law drives her. Kate is alarmed when Reza takes a strange route, saying he wants to show her something. Reza points to a home he bought for Marie as a wedding present.

11:21

The Ambassador and his security officer, Salim, claim they have four suspected members of Second Wave in custody. Satellite photos reveal no security clampdown in their country.

Palmer agrees to the Ambassador's request for American intelligence on the terrorists. The Ambassador leaves in a helicopter but minutes later there is a report it has crashed and there are no survivors.

12:34 Tony and another agent arrive to question Reza at the Warner home. He denies knowing the terrorist Syed Ali, even though the name is in Reza's personal computer files.

Marie is upset. Kate admits she hired a private investigator and uncovered his connection to a terrorist.

12:00—13:00

Jack calls Mason to reveal that Nina Myers – the woman who killed his wife - was commissioned by Wald to blow up CTU.

With her final words before she dies, Paula reveals the database where she had made a copy of the encryption key.

12:09 Jack is at CTU for a debrief when Kim calls and explains the Megan situation.

He again tells her to get to her Aunt Carol's as there may be a nuclear bomb in Los Angeles.

Jack tells her to tell no one but Kim calls her boyfriend Miguel to pick her up at the hospital and tells him about the bomb. She wants to take Megan.

Meanwhile, Nina arrives at CTU and Mason quizzes her about the nuclear bomb. She demands a full Presidential pardon if she helps. Palmer phones Jack and says he must grant Nina a pardon.

Jack realises Mason has been exposed to radiation and is dying. He threatens to call District unless Mason agrees to let Jack handle Nina. Mason reluctantly agrees.

12:21 At the O.C., military advisors speculate on possible bomb targets. The Ambassador arrives along with Roger Stanton, the head of NSA and Rayburn's boss.

Stanton apologises to the President for Rayburn's actions over the CTU bombing. He believes the Ambassador is only there to gain intelligence from the US.

12:07

12:21

13:00-14:00

Jack promises Mason he will put aside his personal anger to get the truth from Nina. She wants to go to Visalia as her contact will tell only her the location of the bomb.

13:09 Jack slams her against the wall and threatens to kill her unless she says the contact's name. Mason orders Jack out of the room. Mason notices Nina is visibly afraid, whilst Jack is calm, so agrees to another five minutes. Jack pulls out a gun and fires shots into the wall past Nina's head. He then aims at her head and she admits her contact is Mamud Faheen.

Faheen had introduced Nina to Wald who wanted her to get schematics for CTU. Nina refuses to give his exact location unless she can go to Visalia. Mason agrees.

Agent Miller will accompany Jack and Nina to Visalia. In the transport van, Jack hands a bottle to Miller. But it is drugged and the agent collapses. Jack cocks his gun and smiles at Nina. A look of fear spreads over her face.

13:35 Ex-wife Sherry asks Palmer about military personnel being evacuated from Los Angeles. He requested no evacuations and asks Lynne to investigate.

NSA chief Stanton reckons the helicopter crash was planned as the Prime Minister was unhappy with his Ambassador working with America. Palmer suggests forces within his own government may be to blame.

Lynne discovers military personnel and resources are evacuating under Stanton's orders. Palmer stops the evacuation.

The President reveals the bomb threat to Sherry who confesses a high level staffer at the Defense Department told her members of his administration are allying against him.

13:43 Reza asks for a lawyer as Tony continues his questioning at the Warner residence. Reza's parents are told government agents are questioning him about alleged terrorist activity. The Naiyeers believe he is being victimised because he is Middle Eastern.

Tony asks Reza about a money transfer to Ali. Reza claims he did the transfers to cover for Bob Warner, Marie's father.

13:54 A doctor warns Gary that Megan has concussion and must remain in hospital for observation. But Gary books two tickets to Mexico and begins to dress Megan.

Gary goes to take a call at the nurses' station. The caller is really Miguel. When Gary returns to the room, Megan is missing.

Kim, Megan and Miguel hide in an examination room. Miguel grabs a flat screen computer monitor then runs to distract security that allows Kim and Megan to escape.

Gary spots the girls outside and is about to hit Kim when Miguel knocks him out with a martial arts kick. They grab Gary's keys and run for his car.

14:00-15:00

Mason calls his estranged son, John, who refuses to visit. Mason has police bring him to CTU where he gives his son the number of a secret bank account where he has stashed a few hundred thousand dollars. He tells his son he is dying and asks him to leave Los Angeles as it is unsafe.

The CTU jet carrying Jack and Nina lands at Davenport Airfield in Visalia and is met FBI agents. Nina says Faheen is at a store called Crescent Collectibles.

Jack and the FBI agents prepare for a raid and Nina warns Faheen will kill himself to protect the terrorists' plan. Nina enters Crescent Collectibles as Jack waits outside – she has a wire attached to her necklace to transmit audio and pictures to Jack.

Michelle is watching and listening at CTU as Nina is taken to a back room. Jack loses contact but Michelle tells him what is happening. Nina tells Faheen she had to pay to get out of prison and needs his help to disappear. Faheen hugs Nina and the audio goes dead. Jack orders the raid and finds Faheen unconscious and Nina gone.

Nina runs to a gated door, but it is locked. As Jack arrives, she drops her gun, turns her back to him and puts her hands on her head. Jack handcuffs her.

14:20 Palmer's Chief of Staff, Novick, arrives at the retreat in Oregon and is surprised to see Sherry. Novick is doubtful

about Sherry's conspiracy story but promises to investigate. Palmer suggests starting with NSA Director Roger Stanton. Lynne and Palmer discuss how to handle the Ron Wieland situation. The reporter has not been seen since being taken into custody. Novick suggests Richard Armus leaks a story about Wieland being away on personal business.

Lynne briefs the President about CTU locating weapons grade nuclear material in a warehouse. He is concerned that Jack is working with Nina Myers.

Lynne meets Palmer and Novick. Lynne tells Sherry she has a provisional security clearance and gives her permission to disclose secrets. Lynne is shocked to learn Stanton is a suspect in a plot against the President. Sherry reveals Stanton and Rayburn had secret meetings with a Senator. Lynne says those meetings have nothing to do with this situation. Palmer still wants to be certain Stanton is not working against them.

14:38 Kate is angry with Reza for implicating Bob to save himself. He claims he told the truth. Tony calls Mason to say Bob Warner is the new suspect. Mason wants Bob and Reza at CTU for further questioning.

Kate calls her private investigator, but gets his boss, Paul Koplin, who she asks for help in accessing her father's private records.

14:53 Police stop Kim and Miguel for speeding but let Miguel off with a warning. As he returns to his squad car the officer notices blood dripping from the trunk. Miguel is stunned when find a woman's body. The policeman pulls his gun, forces Miguel to the ground and calls for backup. Kim recognizes the woman is Carla.

15:00–16:00

The policeman who discovered the body in the boot arrests Kim and Miguel. Kim begs the officer to contact her father, Jack. He speaks to her on the phone and not long afterwards Kim and Miguel are told they are being transferred to CTU. She asks about Megan, insisting the little girl is not taken back to Los Angeles. The policeman pushes Kim to reveal what is going on, and she admits the nuclear bomb story.

15:03 At the retreat, Sherry tells Palmer she will try to persuade reporter Weiland to accept an exclusive on-air interview.

In the holding room, she promises Wieland that if he keeps the rumours quiet he can report from inside the O.C. Wieland will not agree.

Wieland goes live and reports an imminent threat to national security by Middle Eastern and domestic terrorists. He says the President is aware and keeping the problem hush. Palmer wants to know how Wieland escaped and demands to see Armus.

15:20 Nina, Jack and Faheen head back to LA in the CTU jet. Faheen tells Nina he is not afraid to die for his cause.

They talk in Arabic but Michelle translates for Jack. Nina says she can save Faheen's family from being arrested by U.S. forces. Then Nina suddenly cuts Faheen's throat with a shard of gift card she has had hidden in her palm since entering Crescent Collectibles.

Faheen dies and Nina is the only one who knows where the bomb is. She tells Jack to fly to San Diego and will only give him the information when they have landed. Mason accepts her demands.

Suddenly, an explosion rocks the plane and bodies are tossed about the cabin.

15:37

15:31 In the van transporting the nuclear device, Basheer informs Marko and Omar that "Everybody is ready."

They pull over with a flat tyre and Marko sees children playing nearby. He says he can't go through with the plan. Basheer shoots him in the chest. Marko shoots him back and they both fall out of the van dead. Omar doesn't know what to do.

15:40 Tony escorts Reza, Marie and Bob Warner to CTU and tells Mason there is a connection to Syed Ali.

Warner admits working as a consultant for the CIA. His international investment company passes information to an unknown source. Bob says he does not know Ali.

Michelle tells Mason the name Marko Khatami was heard during Faheen's discussion with Nina and she connected it to Ali. Reza denies knowing Khatami.

Meanwhile, Paul Koplin, the boss of private investigator Ralph Burton, arrives at the Warner house. He knows of the files that link Reza to Ali and attaches a transmitter to Bob's computer. Kate notices Koplin is carrying a gun.

Koplin finds records of Reza withdrawing money and a payment to Ali for $475,000. He then uncovers government files that begin to auto-delete. Koplin stops the deletion and the screen fills with ASCII codes. He recognises them as encoded co-ordinate addresses that need government security clearance. He says he will call Tony Almeida.

Two men appear and inject something into Kate and Koplin and put their bodies into a truck.

15:20

16:40

DAY TWO

16:00-17:00

As the CTU jet descends in flames, the pilot tells Jack he is going to crash land. Jack calls Mason with the co-ordinates.

16:08 In the Angeles National Forest, Jack rolls out of the plane's fuselage, and pulls a tree branch from his thigh. Agent Phillips is barely alive. Nina is unconscious and strapped to her seat. Jack finds a flare gun and leads the handcuffed Nina away.

They spot soldiers inspecting the wreckage and one of them shoots Phillips. Nina denies knowing the soldiers. Jack shoots a soldier with the flare gun and grabs his rifle. He fires at the other soldiers then runs off with Nina. Jack unlocks Nina's handcuffs and gives her the ammunition.

Jack fires as she throws him rounds and tells him where to shoot. Nina pockets a rifle clip and gives Jack what she claims is the last round. Jack shoots with his pistol.

A CTU helicopter appears and fires at the soldiers. Nina takes the rifle and loads her hidden clip. Jack puts down his weapon and raises his hands. A Search and Rescue agent commands Nina to drop her gun, but Jack orders the agents to stand down as she knows the location of the bomb. Nina demands to talk to the President.

Michelle shows Mason satellite images that prove a ground-to-air missile shot down the jet.

Wieland tells the media he was detained by the President. Palmer accuses Sherry of having something to do with Wieland's release but Novick shows the President a security tape that reveals Armus releasing Wieland.

The Search and Rescue team phone the O.C. and Nina demands full immunity in advance for murdering Jack! Palmer presses the mute button to speak to Mason who has been listening in. He confirms Nina is the only chance of finding the bomb. Palmer tells Nina that if her information leads to the nuclear device she will be pardoned for Jack's killing.

Nina reveals Ali is in a house in Chatsworth. Jack asks the President to make sure Kim is safe.

Lynne tells the President the press are waiting and hands him his speech. He notices changes and commends her, not knowing they were made by Sherry.

16:21 Mason puts Reza and Bob Warner in the same room in the hope that he might get more information. He reveals to Tony how he was exposed to plutonium.

Mason tells the suspects that weapons grade plutonium was found in a warehouse and a bill for a container delivery from Warner's company was found at the warehouse. He gives them ten minutes to tell the truth.

Tony and Mason listen as Reza questions Bob's involvement, and ask about his supposed CIA activities. Bob tells Reza to be quiet. Reza looks into the security camera and says he can track the order to prove Bob authorised the shipment.

Reza tells Marie that Bob set him up. She is angry with him.

16:43 The police officer tells Kim and Miguel they are being moved to central booking in downtown Los Angeles. His captain overruled CTU's decision to detain them as they are suspects in a capital crime and there are no bomb alerts.

Megan is being taken to Kim's Aunt's house about 100 miles outside of the city.

16:54 In a suburban house, Syed Ali wakens the unconscious Kate Warner. She recognises his name.

Ali takes her to another room where a naked Koplin is tied with his arms over his head. He is aware Warner worked for the CIA and wants to know what the two found on the computer. Kate and Koplin say the files self-deleted.

Ali's assistant, Mohsen, approaches Koplin with a power tool. Koplin's screams are deafened by the soundproof insulation.

Kate says she knows nothing about the computer files. Ali fires three shots at Koplin and orders Mohsen to kill Kate.

16:54

17:32

17:00-18:00

The President admits to the media that there is a terrorist threat. He guarantees there is no cause for alarm.

As Nina holds Jack hostage in the forest, she tells him she only killed his wife Teri because she overheard details of her escape route.

Jack spots a sharpshooter and walks forward to bring Nina into sight where she is shot in the hand. CTU agents take Nina captive. Novick informs the President that CTU have Nina. Palmer says she will be pardoned if they confirm her information.

Jack spots a tattoo of coral snake on a dead soldier's wrist.

He calls Palmer from a helicopter as he makes his way to the address Nina provided and says the tattoo is the signature of an undercover special ops unit under the command of Colonel Samuels at Fort Benning.

NSA Director Stanton tells Palmer he does not know of the Coral Snake unit or Samuels. The President wants Stanton arrested. Sherry has reservations but Novick says Stanton could be holding back the search for the bomb. Palmer asks Novick to find a link between Stanton and Samuels.

Sherry tells Palmer and Novick about a communications network called OPCOM that the CIA used twenty years ago. Stanton resurrected it a month ago. Her source is checking to see if Stanton used OPCOM to contact Samuels.

Stanton gets a cell phone call in the O.C. It is Sherry. She says she told the President about OPCOM and is working her way into having Palmer trust her again. She warns Stanton not to talk about her involvement when he is arrested. If Stanton does as they have planned, he will have power.

17:04 Miguel gets into a fight with a policeman trying to take him and Kim back to LA. In the scuffle he secretly grabs a lighter that falls out of the officer's pocket.

Miguel gets Kim to help him set fire to a bandanna in his pocket. As the officer tries to put out the fire he loses control of the car and it crashes into an embankment.

Kim takes the unconscious officer's keys, unlocks her handcuffs and radios for help. Miguel is badly injured.

Miguel urges her to leave before help arrives. She runs off into the woods as an ambulance approaches.

17:06 Reza takes CTU operatives to the Warner building where Agent Richards boots up Bob's computer. Reza guides him through accessing the invoice files.

Struggling to find a connection between the Warners and Ali, Tony asks Michelle for a list of managers and directors at Warner Investments.

On Bob's computer, Reza uncovers Ali's shipping order. It was entered last January when both of them were in Europe. Someone had been hacking into the system through Reza's laptop.

A shot rings out and Reza looks up to see Marie holding a gun. "I didn't expect you to find anything," she says. Marie shoots him dead.

17:32 Mohsen tells Ali he wants to be certain Kate told everything before he kills her. Ali leaves to pray. Mohsen questions Kate again about Warner's computer.

Outside the house, CTU agents brief Jack and watch two figures on an infrared imager. Mohsen trains his gun on Kate then says something terrible is going to happen that will cause much suffering. Mohsen spots the shadow of a gunman on the roof and fires upwards.

Jack bursts in and shoots Mohsen who begins to foam at the mouth and dies having taken a cyanide pill. Kate tells Jack how she and Koplin were kidnapped. The man who escaped is Syed Ali.

Jack asks Tony for a background check on Kate Warner. Tony explains his investigation into Reza and Bob Warner. Jack reasons the family is involved with the nuclear threat.

Kate says Ali and Mohsen spoke in hushed Arabic tones but she only recognised the word "prayer." Jack looks at his watch and tells an agent to locate the nearest mosque. It is nearly time for Muslim prayer.

18:00-19:00

Agent Richards and Reza lie dead in the Warner offices as Marie wrecks the hard drive in her father's computer. Her cell phone rings. It is Ali, who says the drivers Basheer and Marko are dead and he needs her to retrieve the bomb's trigger from Marko's work locker in Burbank.

Ali enters a mosque for what he believes is his last prayer service. Jack arrives at the mosque with Kate and reveals Ali is a suspect in a nuclear terrorist attack.

A SWAT team set up near the mosque. Kate offers to go in wearing a hijab over her face to see if Ali is inside. As Kate dons the traditional Muslim dress, Jack tells her if she spots Ali, she is to leave the building. He gives her a device that will trigger the SWAT team. Kate spots Ali and returns.

The agents watch as the worshipers leave, but they do not see Ali. The team raid the mosque and find a man engulfed in flames. The dead man is wearing clothes that match Ali's but Jack notices the pants are too short. It is not Ali.

18:08 Novick hears there is not enough evidence to take action against Stanton and advises the President to remove Stanton from his post.

Stanton is arrested by Colonel Lamb and accused of conspiracy to commit treason. Palmer informs Sherry that Stanton is being questioned.

Novick reveals Stanton's last call was to Sanders at the CIA. Palmer tells Stanton he has been connected to the nuclear threat. Stanton denies any knowledge.

Palmer asks Secret Service agent Simmons, who served in a special unit for the CIA, to use any means necessary to extract information from Stanton.

Stanton is restrained in a chair with his bare feet in a tub of water. Holding defibrillator paddles, Simmons asks about his involvement with the bomb. Stanton again denies knowledge, and Simmons zaps him on the temples.

18:20 At CTU, Tony admits to Michelle he is happy about them having a relationship. They are interrupted when Bob Warner becomes violent and demands to be freed. He believes Reza is lying about his involvement with terrorists.

Michelle hears that Reza and the agents guarding him were murdered just after Marie Warner arrived. Tony calls Jack and advises treating Kate as a suspect.

He then tells Warner about Reza's murder and the suspicion that Marie is the killer.

Meanwhile, Marie enters a lumber mill wearing a short brunette wig and approaches the foreman about obtaining something from her boyfriend Marko's locker. She seductively offers to show her appreciation for his help and is able to retrieve the trigger.

18:35 Kim is making her way through the forest when she sees a cougar in the distance. She tries to flee but her ankle gets caught in a snare. The cougar stands on a rock and stares at her.

19:00-20:00

At the mosque, an agent discovers a trap door that was not in the building's plans. Jack goes down into the basement first and arrests Ali. He removes the cyanide capsule from Ali's teeth but not before he has had time to call Marie and give her instructions on what to do if he does not arrive at a rendezvous point.

At CTU, Mason confirms to Bob Warner that his daughter is involved with Ali. Michelle informs Mason Ali has been captured and a burnt fragment of paper was found with his clothes. Jack interrogates Ali who is ready to die for his cause.

They call the last number dialled from Ali's cell phone. Kate recognises Marie's number. Jack tells her about Reza's murder and that Marie is the main suspect.

19:15 Tony directs a rescue team searching for Kimberly in the forest. As Kim tries to free her foot from the trap, a man with a rifle asks how she got there. The man, McRae, releases her.

McRae wraps up Kim's ankle and offers to help her to the ranger's station. Kim doesn't want to go, so he offers to let her stay at his nearby house.

Jack instructs Kate on how to keep Marie on the line so they can trace the phone. They rig it so Kate's number will appear on the caller ID. Marie answers and realises Reza's body has been found.

The techs trace the call to Sylmar, but Marie hangs up and throws the phone out of the car. The phrase "N34" is revealed by experts who examine the charred paper. Tony has Michelle look for links to this code.

Jack asks Ali about "N34". He then turns on video monitors that show Ali's wife and children via satellite from his home. Masked soldiers are tying them up.

Jack threatens to kill his family unless he gets answers. Ali remains silent. Jack is interrupted by a call from the President, who forbids him from killing these people. Jack lets Ali believe he has the full support of the President.

Over a satellite phone, Jack gives instructions to start with Ali's first-born son. A masked soldier pushes the boy's chair over and shoots him. Ali will still not talk.

Jack is about to order the shooting of the next son when Ali caves in. The plan is to detonate the bomb from a plane over downtown. The bomb is at Norton Airfield where all the planes have numbers that begin with the letter "N."

Ali curses Jack for killing his son, but the boy is really alive. The whole shooting had been staged. Jack asks Kate to accompany him to Norton Airfield.

19:51 Lynne approaches Novick and says Sherry Palmer is untrustworthy. She explains Sherry has communicated with Stanton for the last six months even though they claimed to have met that morning.

Lynne has a face-to-face meeting with her unknown source in ten minutes. Novick instructs Lynne to update him after the meeting.

She arrives at a highway rest and is surprised to see Sherry. Sherry says Stanton's conspirators wanted Lynne to connect the situation to her. They want to control the President and have been feeding misinformation about Sherry.

19:59 Marie arrives at an airplane hangar where Omar is waiting with the bomb. She takes out the trigger and he connects it.

19:04

`20:03`

20:00-21:00

Under interrogation Stanton admits being part of a group that wants to make Palmer's defence policy more aggressive. They allowed the bomb to enter America, and permitted Second Wave terrorist to operate. Samuels' special ops forces have been tracking the bomb and plan to stop it being detonated. Stanton reveals the special ops team at Norton Airfield have been out of contact for three hours.

The President orders all agents to Norton Airfield after confirming that's where the bomb is. Mason informs Jack that Coral Snake team, a hostile unit who shot down Jack's plane, will prevent him getting to the bomb.

`20:09` At the airfield, Omar is getting the plane ready to fly the bomb over the city when Marie spots police cars. Jack is met by Steve Goodrich, an agent heading the assault team. Goodrich  shows footprints left by military combat boots that enter a fuel depot but do not leave. Jack and a SWAT team raid the building and find Coral Snake commandos dead, all shot in the forehead.

Novick informs the President six commandoes were found dead. Stanton says there were originally seven soldiers.

Murdoch has now completed work on the scrap of paper and tells Jack the plane is in hangar MD7. Omar climbs into a Cessna plane as Marie opens the hangar doors. Jack and the SWAT team spot the plane. Jack has the Hummer he is riding in pull alongside the Cessna and shoots Omar. The bomb is

inside but the nuclear specialist realises it is a fake.

Palmer visits Stanton again and gives him one final chance. Stanton tells the President to ask Sherry.

`20:30` Kim limps behind McRae through the forest but refuses to return to Los Angeles to see a doctor. When she admits the terrorist nuclear threat, McRae says he always suspected something like this would happen.

McRae reveals he has built a bomb shelter, and it is full of weapons and ammunition. He boasts he would be one of the few survivors from an explosion.

A park ranger arrives and asks McRae if has spotted a teenage girl. He explains she was arrested for kidnap and murder. McRae denies seeing her. Kim tells McRae she is innocent. McRae panics when he discovers all Los Angeles radio stations have gone static. A station outside the county reports a flash in the sky. They both enter the shelter.

`20:43` Novick has discovered Stanton was working with a Senator from Michigan named Gluck. Palmer suggests they bring in Sherry as she is close to Gluck. He tells Novick to give her access to the O.C.'s secure databases.

Sherry arrives and is given access cards to the facility. Palmer asks Sherry to find whatever she can about Stanton's relationship with Senator Gluck.

`20:03`

`20:17`

21:42

21:00–22:00

Jack asks for a translator so he can quiz Omar. He then calls Mason and asks for a reverse-time satellite to track the delivery of the decoy. Mason is clearly struggling with radiation sickness and Jack pleads with him to stand down. Mason reveals there was a seventh commando.

Omar begins to say something in Arabic, so Jack goes to get Kate from an airport room to see if she can help. Kate translates that Omar claims he took part in the attack as Ali promised to pay his family. He knows nothing about a second bomb.

Kate enters the building where people are being checked by security and spots Marie leaving by a back door. She tells a guard to radio Jack and follows Marie. But her sister pulls a gun on her and demands her CTU badge. A shot rings out as Jack hits Marie in the arm. Marie is handcuffed to a chair and Jack says when she tells them where the bomb is she will receive treatment.

She is given painkillers so Jack can get her to talk. When they wear off Marie finally gives in and tells Jack the bomb is in a suitcase in a green van and going to the Arco Towers. It will detonate in three hours. Jack is convinced she is lying.

Jack spots gunfire ahead as the CTU radio reports one hostile is down. Goodrich directs him to the bomb in an Army duffel bag. Jack orders an evacuation as the bomb could go off at any second.

21:04 The President informs Sherry he knows about Stanton bringing the bomb into the country. Sherry denies working with Stanton and says she only met him that afternoon. She admits to being approached by Stanton but only went along with him to gain his confidence.

Novick sets up a video call for the President with Steve Hillenburg, a CIA operative at Langley. He confirms Sherry contacted him four months ago because Stanton was trying to recruit her to undermine the Administration.

21:17 Mason meets Carrie Turner, the programmer who replaces Paula Schaeffer, and tells her to report to Tony and Michelle. She used to be Michelle's boss at District.

Mason admits to Tony he is too unwell to continue and says he is now Director. Tony explains the situation to CTU staff and says they must get through this crisis.

He pulls up a file on special ops soldier Jonathan Wallace, who is believed to be the seventh commando.

21:55 In the bomb shelter, McRae puts on headphones for his shortwave radio and hears the Los Angeles radio stations. He pulls out the antennae connection and tells Kim there is only static. But Kim finds a television and discovers all the stations are fully operational. She realises she is in danger.

Kim persuades McRae to let her go and he hands her a flashlight and a gun and points her to a trail.

22:00-23:00

Mason arrives at Norton Airfield to learn the bomb's trigger is tamperproof and will explode in 55 minutes. The President is informed and a plane requested to fly the bomb out of the city, to the desert or the ocean.

The desert is chosen as the best option but the bomb must be delivered to a precise point. The only way of doing this in the civilian plane would be for the pilot to go down with the craft.

Several men volunteer but Mason says he wants to undertake the task as he is dying anyway. Jack refuses as he is worried Mason could black out before the mission is over.

As Jack boards the Cessna, Kate warns it is equipped with a clock synchronized to the bomb's timer. Novick informs the President the plane is in the air.

Jack senses movement, draws his gun and sees Mason. He hands Jack a parachute and says he will now take over. Jack agrees and gives him instructions. Jack will jump four minutes before impact. Tony arranges a helicopter to pick up Jack in the desert.

22:17 CTU agents deliver a suitcase full of Ali's personal effects to Tony. Yusuf Auda, a visiting intelligence liaison from the Arab country suspected of harbouring the Second Wave terrorists, also arrives. Tony orders Michelle to ensure Yusuf

A recording is found on Ali's hard drive of a conversation months ago between Ali and high-ranking officials of three Middle Eastern governments. It confirms they supplied the bomb.

Tony informs the President who is concerned that Division will have notified the Pentagon and other agencies. Palmer warns Novick they could soon be at war.

Aboard Air Force One, General Bowden from the Joint Chiefs, talks to the President about retaliation. The military know the three Middle Eastern countries that funded the terrorists. Plans for war are underway. Palmer warns that military action must not go ahead without his direct authorisation.

22:21 Kim flags down a car on a deserted road. She is wary of the driver, fires her gun and he drives off. A woman called Anna gives Kim a lift and lets her use her cell phone. Tony patches Kim through to Jack on the plane. Jack tells her he is on a suicide mission.

22:57 As Mason pilots the Cessna toward Ground Zero, Jack parachutes to the ground and hides behind a rock as he hears an explosion in the distance. Kim looks up to see a faint glow. Palmer watches as a mushroom cloud

23:00—00:00

23:59

Yusuf Auda is again brushed off when he asks Tony why he isn't allowed to take part in the investigation. Tony asks Carrie to handle the audio verification of Ali's Cyprus tape about the countries that hired him.

Audio techs believe the voices have not been tampered with. Michelle says Ali denies the conversations took place and claims he was in Berlin. She believes the tape has been doctored. Carrie disagrees.

Ali is carried out of CTU as Jack returns from the desert. Michelle tells Jack she fears the President is planning military action based on Ali's recording. She wants Jack to interrogate him again.

Jack admits to Ali that they staged the killing of his son, and then asks about the Cyprus recording. Ali says that what he told Michelle was true. A single shot from a sniper rings out. Ali falls dead.

Tony and Jack know the leak about Ali's move could have come from anywhere in the intelligence community. Tony believes one of the three countries on the recording is responsible.

The President is told of the Cyprus tape and calls for an emergency session of Congress to ask for a declaration of war. In a video link with his Joint Chiefs of Staff, he hears surgical strikes can start that day but it will take eight to ten weeks to get troops into the Middle East.

23:22

Deputy Prime Minister Barghouti calls and pledges his country's support to Palmer against Second Wave. He asks the President not to make a hasty response.

Jack calls the President and says Ali has been assassinated, which suggests the Cyprus recording is fake. Palmer informs Novick they may be acting too hastily in starting a war.

23:34 Kim goes to a store for help but Frank Davies, who works there, locks himself and Kim in the restroom.

23:45 Jack asks Yusuf if it is possible the tape may have been compromised. Yusuf says nothing. An unknown man calls Jack and claims he planted the tape and shot Ali. He demands Kate Warner is taken to a warehouse.

Jack tells Michelle he may be able to prove the tape is a fake. Michelle goes to a holding room where Baker is debriefing Kate. She gets him out of the room so Jack can slip in. Yusuf and Carrie see this happen. Carrie phones Tony.

Tony stops Jack at gunpoint but Jack takes away the gun and knocks out Tony. Jack grabs Kate and leaves.

23:52 Kim hears someone banging on the door. Davies tells the man, Garcia, that the store is closed. Garcia smashes a shopping cart through the glass. He then takes Kim's gun.

Davies turns on the news at Garcia's request and there are reports about the nuclear bomb. The police arrive and in a scuffle Garcia accidentally fires Kim's gun. Davies falls down bleeding. Garcia takes Kim hostage.

`00:19`

Snake. Samuels had called Jack "a born killer."

Carrie tells Tony she saw Michelle and Jack speaking before he took Kate. Tony has Carrie put a filter on Michelle's communications to see if Jack contacts her.

Carrie listens in when Michelle receives a phone call from a man named Danny. He asks if he and the children are safe but she won't give him any information. Danny threatens to call Carrie to find out what's going on. Danny admits he thinks Carrie is a bitch and hangs up. Carrie deletes the recording.

Yusuf brings in Kate who is put in the trunk of a

car. Yusuf has put a tracker on the car. The car windshield shatters as gunfire comes from above the warehouse. Wallace, Jack and Yusuf return fire.

`00:35` At the convenience store, Davies dies of his gunshot wound.

The police put Garcia's wife on the phone, and he tells her to leave the city. He then orders the police to take her to Monterey before he will release Kim.

As Garcia talks to the policeman, Kim locks herself in a back room and the police help her escape. The SWAT team raid the store. Kim hears shots and a medical team is called.

`00:56` The President, Lynne and Novick arrive in Los Angeles and Palmer is put through to vice President Jim Prescott in Washington. Prescott is about to meet the British ambassador and explain about the retaliation.

CTU Director Chappelle, Novick and Lynne talk to Prescott via videophone. Prescott reveals the ambassador is annoyed the United States is planning an attack without co-ordinating with Britain. Novick believes Palmer is capable of making the right decision and is committed to military action.

00:00-01:00

As Jack and Kate escape from CTU, he tells her a world war could start over the fake tape. The man who claims to have forged this evidence wants Kate.

Carrie tells Tony she thinks Michelle helped Jack as she distracted another agent. Michelle denies the accusation.

As he drives towards a warehouse in Studio City, Jack realises he is being trailed. He pulls his gun on the driver – Yusuf who offers to help Jack.

`00:19` Jack arrives at the warehouse and tells Kate to remain in the car. Inside, Captain Jonathan Wallace, the seventh commando who took out his own platoon, admits planting the recording.

The people who hired him control oil in the Caspian Sea, and a war in that region would quadruple their wealth. The same people tried to kill Wallace an hour ago.

As he talks to Jack, Wallace secretly taps his foot against a plug in its socket underneath the table and a neon sign outside flickers. That is the signal for a man to grab Kate. But before he can, Yusuf hits the man over the head.

Jack's cell phone rings and he hands it to Wallace. Yusuf tells the commando his man has been knocked out. Wallace won't give his evidence to Jack unless Kate organises his escape through Warner Industries. Wallace gathers his weapons and with no other choice, Jack radios Yusuf to bring Kate in.

Wallace reveals he was at Fort Benning when Samuels unsuccessfully tried to recruit Jack for Coral

`00:46`

01:55

01:00-02:00

Jack pulls Kate from the trunk of the car and enters the warehouse with Wallace, as Yusuf darts into an alley. Wallace believes shooters have been sent by his employers.

Jack calls Michelle's cell phone and she warns him agency phones are being monitored. He needs her to check infrared satellite images to find out how many men are surrounding the warehouse.

01:15 Carrie questions what Michelle is doing on the satellite. She shows Tony the data Michelle has been collecting and assumes Jack can be found at the co-ordinates. He isn't aware Michelle covered her tracks with hundreds of searches.

Michelle goes to the restroom and sends Jack a map of the warehouse and the location of the shooters from her PDA.

Jack and Wallace work out an escape route. Jack arms Kate and then radios Yusuf with the locations of the gunmen. Yusuf throws smoke grenades into the alley and fires toward the roof. Kate is separated from the group as Yusuf goes for the car. She spots a sniper and shoots him. Wallace follows but is hit in the neck by a shot.

Tony gets reports about gunfire in Studio City and links it to a location Michelle has searched. Michelle dials Jack and hands the phone to Tony. Jack says he was ordered by the President to prove the recording is a fake.

Kate phones ahead to the airport to prepare a cargo transport but Wallace loses consciousness. Jack plugs into the car's GPS to find the nearest medical centre. But Wallace tells Jack he's not going to make it and

whispers that the original files for the Cyprus recording are on a memory chip. Before he can finish he dies, saying "it's inside".

Jack notices a light box holding Wallace's x-ray and spots a shadow at the bottom of the rib cage. There is a stitch scar. Jack grabs a scalpel, cuts the body and grabs the blood-covered microchip.

01:30 Palmer and his staff watch news reports about violence erupting across America following the nuclear bomb. Bombers are due to reach the Middle East in less than five hours. Palmer orders no pre-emptive strikes.

Novick reveals that groups in Marietta outside Atlanta, Georgia are joining forces in racial attacks against Middle-Eastern people. The President enforces a curfew and orders the National Guard to make arrests.

The National Guard shoot rubber bullets and two people are killed, one a young Middle Eastern boy.

01:42 Kim admits to police she is a murder suspect who escaped police custody. Deputy Raynes takes Kim to the Sheriff's station and hands her to Sergeant Amis who asks Kim about Megan Matheson's kidnapping. Kim says Megan was being abused.

Amis reveals Gary Matheson has confessed to killing his wife Carla. Kim calls Tony at CTU and asks for help. She is shocked her father is still alive. Kim calls hospital and speaks to Miguel who says he doesn't want to see her any more. He doesn't tell her his right leg has been amputated.

DAY TWO

02:00-03:00

Yusuf examines the microchip under a magnifying glass and discovers a transponder. He is able to remove it without damaging the audio files. Jack calls Tony to say they are heading to CTU with a chip containing the evidence.

02:06 The men hunting Wallace arrive at the clinic. Jack takes the tracker and tells Yusuf and Kate to meet him nearby. If he is not there in fifteen minutes, they must deliver the chip to CTU. Jack is tracked on a handheld GPS monitor as he leaves the clinic and is shot with a taser by Ronnie Stark.

Jack is searched with a metal detector as the men search for the chip. Stark receives a call from Peter Kingsley, in a helicopter over Los Angeles. He offers Jack money for the chip. He refuses. Stark dips a scalpel in ammonia and slices into Jack's abdomen. Stark opens another wound in Jack's side and then burns Jack where he has been cut.

Jack is hit twice more with the taster and his body goes slack. His captors fear he is dead and cut off his bindings.

As Yusuf is about to drive to CTU with the chip a group of men pull him from the car and accuse him of being an Arab who bombed the United States. He warns them off with his gun but another man hits him from behind with a brick. Kate is also attacked.

02:13 Palmer tells the Joint Chiefs and Cabinet he is awaiting Jack to deliver evidence that the recording is a fake.

After hearing Jack has the chip, Palmer wants to call off the attack. Novick says his lack of response to the nuclear weapon exploding may make him look weak.

Lynne asks Novick about a meeting called by the Vice President. Novick is secretly meeting with Defense Department official Jesper Isberg. Lynne insists on being at the meeting.

Novick meets Lynne on the fifth floor and asks her if she knows Section 4 of the 25th Amendment, where the cabinet can vote to remove a President from office if he is unfit for his duties. The Vice President would become acting President.

Novick asks Lynne where she stands on Palmer's decision. She does not agree with the President but is loyal and believes Prescott should be charged with treason. Novick has Isberg lock her in the room.

02:30 Michelle asks Carrie to allow her to run analysis on the chip Jack is bringing in. Carrie refuses and Michelle accuses her of trying to sabotage her work.

Tony asks what is going on. Michelle admits she and Carrie were friends at Division. Her brother Danny left his wife and children for Carrie, who then dumped him. Danny lost his job and his family, and attempted suicide.

Danny arrives at CTU to see Michelle and wants to apologise for yelling at her. Danny spots Carrie and puts his hands around her throat.

Chappelle phones to says he is on his way to CTU with key people from Division to help out.

03:00-04:00

The clinic doctor is ordered at gunpoint to administer drugs and revive Jack. O'Hara shoots Stark and demands the chip. As O'Hara takes a call from Kingsley, the doctor starts to untie his ropes. But his captor returns and orders the medic to inject Beroglide into Jack to paralyse his diaphragm.

03:25 As the doctor prepares another syringe, he gives Jack a nod. O'Hara leans over Jack and the doctor slams the syringe into O'Hara's back. Jack grabs O'Hara's gun and shoots the other henchmen. He asks O'Hara who was on the phone and gives the name Peter Kingsley before Jack shoots him.

Jack takes O'Hara's phone and calls Michelle. He tries to tell her about the chip but she can only hear static. Tony wants the call traced.

The men who attacked Yusuf find the chip and take it with his belongings. Kate offers them money for the chip and they drive off in the car with her. Jack arrives after his ordeal at the clinic and just before he dies Yusuf tells him his attackers have taken Kate to her house.

Kate takes the men to a safe in her home where they find cash and a diamond bracelet. She runs off as Jack appears and shoots one of them. Jack chases the other two but one threatens to smash the chip.

Meanwhile, Kingsley is in his office when Alexander Trepkos enters and says "Max" is unhappy as their project depends on military action.

03:35 Novick tells Vice President Prescott that Palmer is unaware of what is happening and that he has Lynne out of the way.

Novick asks the President to change his mind about delaying the war. Palmer thanks Novick for standing by him.

Lynne, who is attempting to escape the fifth floor room, finds a blowtorch and starts a fire that sets off an alarm. As Isberg enters, Lynne hits him with a fire extinguisher and runs. She falls down some stairs and is knocked unconscious.

Palmer phones the Vice President but is told he's unavailable. The President wants Lynne to go over his statement to the media and Novick says he will find her. Novick then calls Prescott from a satcom phone and warns Palmer is becoming suspicious as the Vice President hasn't returned his calls.

Palmer and Novick watch as Lynne is taken to hospital suffering from concussion. She raises a weak hand and points toward Novick.

Prescott tells the Cabinet that the purpose of their meeting is to decide whether Palmer is fit to continue as President.

03:42 At CTU, Michelle tells Tony that Jack called from a cell phone between Studio City and Encino. Tony does not want Michelle to use the satellite as Chappelle could find out what they are doing. Carrie secretly watches them speak.

Carrie warns Tony that Chappelle will not be happy with time used on finding Jack. She says she will stay quiet if he gives her Michelle's job.

Tony calls Chappelle and says Carrie is blackmailing him for promotion. She tells him they are searching for Jack but Chappelle dismisses Carrie and rebukes Tony.

03.55

`04:20`

the President. He says Palmer was indecisive about military action and hoped to avoid war by proving an American was behind the bomb.

Palmer says he did order the torture, that Stanton confessed to knowing about the bomb and gave information about the Coral Snake team.

`04:31` Jack interrupts Palmer's conference to reveal the chip is damaged and that a man named Peter Kingsley is part of a group who want a war so they can control Middle East oil.

Palmer returns to his meeting where the Secretary of State uses his casting vote to remove the President. Prescott takes control.

04:00-05:00

Jack breaks down the door to Kate's bathroom and grabs the chip off one of the men. He then calls Michelle to say he is unable to read the chip and wants a background check on Peter Kingsley.

Michelle helps Jack with access to the chip but he only gets a screen of numbers and symbols. He sends the data to Michelle for retrieval.

Although Tony and Michelle did not find audio files they discover junk code and trace it to a hacker named Alex Hewitt.

`04:05` Palmer discovers the bombers did not return to their bases as he ordered. Novick invites him to the conference room where he sees cabinet members and Vice President Prescott on a video link.

Prescott tells Palmer they are invoking the 25th Amendment to take away his powers. The Secretary of State says Jack has not brought evidence to prove the Cyprus recording is fake.

Prescott brings in the reporter Wieland who explains how he was detained by the Secret Service after he investigated a possible terrorist attack. Wieland believed Palmer was not in control of the situation.

`04:23` Palmer asks Novick how long he has known about Prescott's plan to get him out of office. Novick claims to be on the President's side.

NSA head Stanton appears on a monitor and describes how he was tortured under orders from

`04:23`

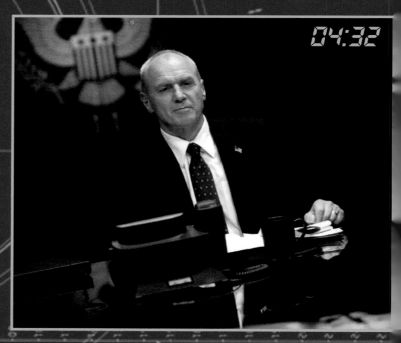

`04:32`

05:00-06:00

Sherry Palmer has arrived at Hewitt's loft with her bodyguard. As Jack listens in she says Kingsley's men must have taken anything that was important.

Jack knocks out the bodyguard and asks Sherry what she is doing there. She claims to be working on Palmer's behalf. Jack fires his gun at the wall and she admits Hewitt is an audio technician who was hired by Kingsley to fake the recording. Kingsley wants to start a war with the Middle East because of his oil interests there.

Jack realises someone is hiding in the room and fires more shots which lead to a frightened Hewitt revealing himself.

Sherry admits she only wanted revenge on her ex-husband and Kingsley told her the bomb would not be detonated. She asked for Hewitt's help to remove the connection between her and Kingsley. Sherry promises Hewitt full immunity and tells Jack that Hewitt will testify by demonstrating the audio technology.

Jack phones Tony at CTU and is updated on the Palmer situation. He asks for a helicopter to pick up Hewitt. But Chappelle refuses. As Hewitt prepares to make another sample of the Cyprus recording, Jack guarantees the hacker's safety.

05:39 Accompanied by a police officer, Kim enters the Matheson house. Gary Matheson spots the officer but doesn't realise Kim is there and she is unaware of his presence.

Gary packs money, a passport and drugs. Kim hears a noise and calls for the officer. She spots him lying face down outside and notices Gary downstairs.

Gary runs upstairs and finds Kim in the attic. She is able to knock him out with a can and grab his gun and cell phone.

Kim calls CTU and is put through to Jack. She says Matheson has killed the officer and her father tells her to shoot Gary. Jack calls Kate and asks her to pick up his daughter.

05:43 A military advisor briefs Prescott on the bombers' location. He orders the attack to go ahead. Novick asks Palmer for the war key codes. A military officer confirms the codes using a portable scanner.

Palmer explains his situation to Agent Pierce and asks for help in contacting Jack. Tony gets a call from Palmer on a satellite phone secure line and patches the call through to Jack. He tells the President he has Hewitt and Sherry is with him.

As the call ends, Novick takes the satellite phone away from Palmer and Pierce is arrested. Michelle and Tony lure Chappelle to a holding room and use chloroform to render him unconscious.

Tony sends Michelle to arrange the helicopter and phones Jack who asks for the Attorney General to be contacted as Sherry wants to cut a deal.

05:56 Meanwhile in the loft, Hewitt makes a run for a hidden door as Jack is on the phone. He stabs Sherry with a screwdriver. Sherry lies on the ground bleeding, but Jack goes after Hewitt who has gone into a darkened tunnel.

06:21

06:00-07:00

Jack chases Hewitt through the secret tunnel and promises to keep him alive if he helps prevent the war. Hewitt escapes onto the roof and the two face each other with guns drawn. Jack is forced to fire, wounding Hewitt in the leg. He falls over the ledge onto another landing. Jack sees blood pouring from Hewitt's head.

Tony calls Jack to say Chappelle has been removed and that he should contact Michelle in the field on a remote access.

At CTU, Brad Hammond has arrived from Division and locks down the building. Carrie finds Chappelle locked in a room.

Chappelle orders the return of the chopper that has gone for Jack and Hewitt. When the hacker dies on the roof Jack calls Michelle and ask for an interface with Hewitt's computer.

He returns to the loft and discovers Sherry's wounds are minor and asks her to tell Kingsley she can deliver Hewitt as he is unaware the hacker is dead. Sherry is to offer Hewitt to Kingsley in exchange for the evidence that implicates her.

06:05 From his office, Kingsley speaks to a man named Max and assures him the war will increase their oil holdings. A woman named Eve informs Kingsley that Hewitt was not at his loft when they went to find him. He calls Max back and guarantees Hewitt will be found and eliminated.

06:19 Counsellor Brian Jacobs arrives to see Palmer and explains he can appeal the cabinet's decision. Palmer says Kingsley is the man who manipulated the evidence.

Novick gives Jacobs access to intelligence databases in order to make the connection to Kingsley. Novick visits Palmer and says U.S. stealth bombers are over Turkey's airspace, but the country's Prime Minister will not grant a flyover without a personal request from the President. Palmer agrees.

06:34 Michelle connects to Hewitt's computer and finds a programme that can generate any voice. She retrieves a taped phone call between Hewitt and Sherry from the previous night and samples it. CTU agents raid Michelle's van as Jack spots the programme on Hewitt's monitor.

Michelle is led away in handcuffs and taken with Tony to a CTU holding room. Tony insists on taking the blame.

Sherry calls Kingsley and demands the tapes of their conversations in return for Hewitt. Kingsley wants to speak with Hewitt. She holds the receiver to a computer speaker and Jack plays back Hewitt's generated voice. Kingsley suggests a neutral meeting place on Figueroa Street but as he suspects a set up arranges shooters to be present. He tells Eve he will see her in another country then stabs her.

As they head for the meet, Sherry notices Jack is in difficulties. Before she can act he winces and the car swerves off the road into a riverbed basin.

07:00–08:00

Sherry helps Jack out of the crashed car and they stagger away with the audio equipment. A driver stops to offer help but Jack takes his car at gunpoint and lets Sherry drive.

Attorney Jacobs shows Novick a file on Kingsley. It proves he called Coral Snake member Jonathan Wallace, who killed his own men, in the past few hours.

Novick calls Chappelle and orders Jack to be located and given help. Tony and Michelle offer to help Chappelle when he drops the charges against them. Jack is told Kate and Kim are safe at CTU and Chappelle says he is now operating with full support.

Kingsley is expecting the meeting at the Los Angeles Coliseum and Jack can't wait for support. He asks for audio voiceprints of Kingsley and Sherry for authentication. Chappelle grants a live audio feed to the President and sends a SWAT team.

07:19 Jack wires up Sherry with a transmitter when they arrive at the Coliseum. Michelle matches Sherry's voice to her voiceprint. As Sherry heads for the meeting, a sudden pain grips Jack in the chest.

Novick informs Prescott about the Second Wave link and Kingsley and reveals Jack is trying to get a live audio confession from Kingsley. The audio feed is relayed to the White House and to Palmer in Los Angeles.

Palmer is shocked at Sherry's involvement. Novick explains Sherry was recruited by Kingsley, but is now helping Jack.

A sniper aims at Sherry as she enters the arena. She is approached by Kingsley and his guards. Kingsley whispers into a radio for his sharpshooter to wait until they have Hewitt. Sherry says Hewitt is safely hidden.

Kingsley admits using her to ignite the nuclear bomb. She demands a safe haven in return for Hewitt. Michelle confirms Kingsley's voice matches up.

Sherry hands a cell phone to Kingsley and says she will call with Hewitt's location when she is free. He hands over the recordings. She also wants the Cyprus recording. Kingsley can't understand why she needs that tape as Hewitt forged the recording.

07:54

Kingsley is suspicious and instructs his sniper to fire. But his sharpshooter has gone and Jack appears in his place with the sniper's rifle. He shoots dead a guard and yells for Sherry to run. Kingsley fires at Jack.

Jack takes out all but one of Kingsley's men. He leaves the tower, grabs Sherry and hides. As he kills the last guard, a strong pain in the chest causes Jack to stumble to the ground as Kingsley approaches. He reaches for his attacker's gun, but it is empty. Kingsley raises his gun – but shots ring out from a CTU helicopter and he falls dead.

07:47 The military attack stops and Palmer is reinstated as President. He refuses to accept the resignations of Prescott or the cabinet members who voted against him. Novick is relieved from his post.

Meanwhile, a man named Trepkos phones Max to say Kingsley is dead and the President called off the war. Max says a new plan will start today and calls someone else with the go-ahead.

07:52 Chappelle reinstates Tony who thanks Michelle for standing by him. As he waits to go to hospital, Jack sees Kate and Kim arrive at the Coliseum.

Palmer announces the nation is safe and as he walks through a cheering crowd a woman reaches out her hand. Mandy, who was hired by Ira Gaines the previous year to assassinate Palmer, holds his hand.

She leaves the crowd and in private uses tongs to peel off a layer of substance from her right palm. She then places the film into a metal container. She phones Max to say "It's done."

Palmer looks at his right hand and sees the flesh is eaten away. His breath shortens and he falls to the ground gasping for air.

07:04

WEAPONS AND TECH

Your guide to great gear, amazing gizmos and electronic wizardry used by agents and villains in 24

ASCII CODE

The most common format for text files used on computers and the Internet, this stands for American Standard Code for Information Interchange. Private Eye Paul Koplin saw lots of ASCII code appear on a computer screen in Series Two when he accessed Bob Warner's computer.In an ASCII file, each symbol and character is represented with a binary number (a string of seven Os or 1s). Most computers use ASCII codes so they can transfer data from one computer to another. ASCII was developed between 1963 and 1968 and is still in use today. Windows NT and 2000 use a newer system called Unicode.

INFRARED IMAGING

Infrared imaging detects heat radiation that is given off by anything with a temperature.Even items that might appear very cold can give off heat radiation. The human body at normal temperature gives off one of the strongest signals around.In infrared imaging, objects that appear as red areas are the warmest, followed by yellow, green and then blue.

STUN GUNS AND TASERS

Police first used stun guns in the early 1970s so they could stop violent criminals.

Battery-powered, they issue short shocks that cause the victim's muscles to contract when the gun touches them.

Taser guns work in a similar way but by firing charged electrodes at the victim from up to 20 feet. Wires on the electrode attach to clothing and the shock is then sent like a normal stun gun. Stun guns are often used as weapons of torture as they leave little trace of attack.

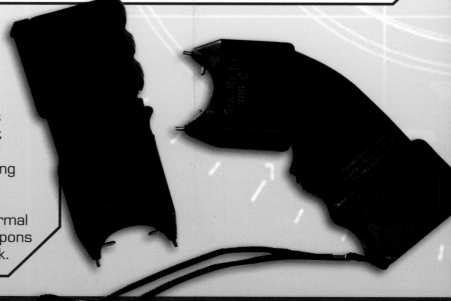

MOBILE RECORDING

Listening in to what the bad guys are up to is vital to stay one step ahead of the game. Forget having to get close enough to slip a bug into their pockets – now it can also be done at distance with special electronic listening devices.

CTU agents have access to mobile video monitoring systems. These are just like souped up versions of your webcam - but let agents hide them in very small places to they can monitor their opponents withouth being seeing. The filming can be relayed back to a nearby van which can also send imagery back to the CTU itself.

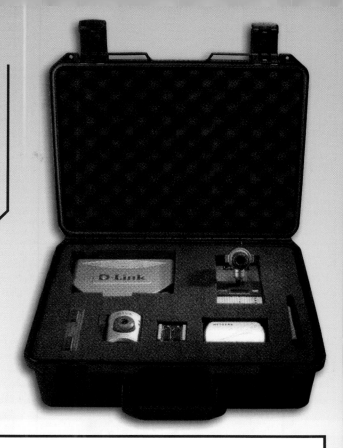

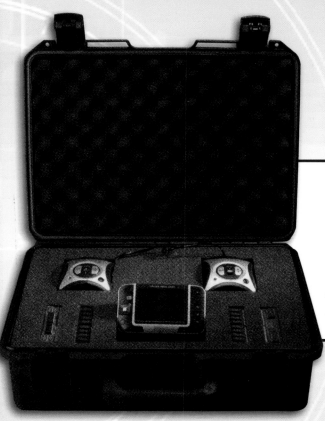

MOBILE VIEWING

A small LCD monitor is used by CTU field teams to view imagery. A small hand-held device can even be used to operate cameras at distance and relay images back to a 4.5in screen.

Even if they don't speak a word their actions might tell you all you need to know to get the edge or foil a bomb attack. Today's digital equipment means you could even lip read what they say from miles away.

RECORDING INTEROGATIONS

Interrogations in the field must be recorded and agents document this with special equipment they carry in a case. This incluces a Panasonic VDR-D300 DVD camcorder and a Logitech Internet camera which can be used to stream imagery in real-time to CTU.

But the recordings can also give away a lot more vital information! Nina Myers was recorded with video cameras and digital audio, but also had wires attached to see her reaction to vital questions. Interrogators can watch for small changes in a person – like eye movements – to see if they are telling the truth.

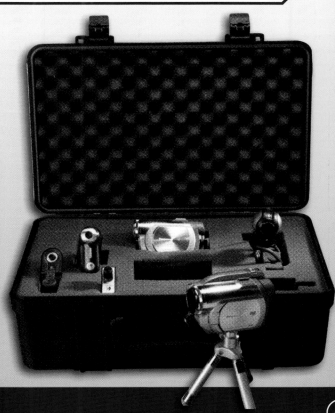

DAY TWO: QUIZ

Test your knowledge of 24 with this quiz. Is your memory for detail as sharp as Jack Bauer's? Answers are on page 126.

01: How is CTU's Special Agent in Charge, George Mason, injured in the field?

(A) Shot (B) Stabbed (C) Poisoned

02: What is the name of the child that Kim cares for?

(A) Melanie (B) Megan (C) Melissa

04: Who is the leader of Coral Snake?

(A) Syed Ali

(B) Jonathan Wallace

(C) Roger Stanton

03: Who was granted a full presidential pardon?

(A) Nina Myers

(B) Sherry Palmer

(C) Syed Ali

05: How are members of Coral Snake identified?

(A) S-shaped tattoo

(B) Snake tattoo

(C) Snake-shaped scar

06: Where does the first scene of the season take place?

(A) Los Angeles, USA

(B) Seoul, South Korea

(C) Beirut, Lebanon

07: Which medical problem does Jack develop after being held by terrorists?

(A) Heart condition

(B) Collapsed lung

(C) Septicaemia

09: What nationality was Max, the arms dealer?

(A) British

(B) German

(C) French

08: Where was the fake recording from?

(A) Greece

(B) Turkey

(C) Cyprus

10: Which airfield did the plane carrying the bomb take off from?

(A) Newton

(B) Norton

(C) Nesdon

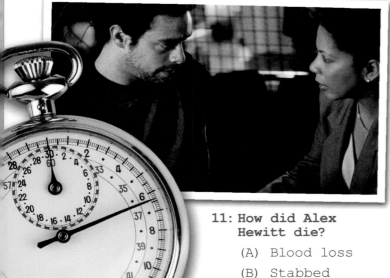

11: How did Alex Hewitt die?

(A) Blood loss

(B) Stabbed

(C) Suicide

12: What is the name of the Vice-President who invoked the 25th amendment?

(A) Alan Prescott

(B) Paul Prescott

(C) Jim Prescott

DAY THREE

TIMELINE:
Three years after Day Two

THREAT:
Terrorists threaten to release a deadly virus in Los Angeles unless one of their number is freed from prison.

MISSION:

Can Jack track the terrorists and stop the virus?

Will a hotel's guest die after being exposed to the virus?

Who is the mystery buyer of the deadly disease?

Has Jack cracked and sided with the terrorists?

13:00-13:00

13:09

13:00-14:00

Inside a van being driven through Los Angeles men prepare a small bomb. With gloved hands, the men place a dead body onto the ground and attach the bomb to the door of the National Health Services facility. A security guard sees the blown off door and find a decomposed body.

A Hazmat team encases the body that has a piece of duct tape on its chest that carries the name of Dr. Sunny Macer. She recognises a virus on the body as a strain her group has been simulating.

CTU Director Tony Almeida's wife, Michelle, puts through a call from Dr Macer who informs him about the body and the virus. He informs Jack Bauer.

13:02 Jack Bauer enters a federal holding facility in Downey with his Field Ops partner, Agent Chase Edmunds. District Attorney Luis Annicon tells Jack that prisoner Ramon Salazar will give up terrorist cells he deals with for a reduced prison sentence.

Jack has spent the last year infiltrating Salazar's drug ring in order to bring down associated terrorists. Salazar's lawyer, Shaye, hands him a pen to sign the deal but he uses it to stab Shaye in the throat.

As they leave, Chase asks Jack how he is doing. "You know what I'm talking about," he says. Jack takes a call from Kate Warner who says she misses him. He hangs up.

Tony receives a call from Larry Hertzog at Langley. He needs to know if Tony will accept the job offered to him.

Michelle instructs Jack's daughter Kimberly, now a low-level analyst at CTU, to do a global capability search for terrorist cells. CTU analyst Adam Kaufman is asked for an ID analysis of the body. He is not happy when Kim is told to assist him.

Jack and Chase enter the Field Operations office at CTU where Chloe O'Brian, Jack's co-ordinator, is checking for links with the dead body and Salazar. As she leaves, Jack bends over in agony.

Dr. Macer briefs Tony and Michelle on test results from the decomposed body as Jack listens on teleconference. The virus has been engineered to kill more rapidly. It could infect thousands of people within two days. Over a million people will die in the first week.

In the ITS room Kim meets Chase and says it's time to admit to her father that they have been dating. Chase wants to do it himself. But when he gets to Jack, Chase sees he looks unwell and is acting erratically. Tony calls them to a meeting where he plays back an anonymous tip phoned to the FBI.

The caller says his group has three pulmonary immuno virus and demand Salazar's freedom within six hours. If their demands are not met the virus will be released.

Jack suspects Salazar's brother Hector is responsible. He knows that questioning Salazar won't work. Michelle reports that the body is David Goss, a street drug dealer in East L.A. who was once an informant.

13:40 At the Salazar Ranch in Las Nieves, Northern Mexico, Ramon's brother Hector kisses his girlfriend Claudia as his cell phone rings. A technician named Gael watches camera surveillance from the Health Services building and reports that the body has been found.

Hector looks into a giant pit where a lorry is dumping decomposed dead bodies. Claudia's father is the foreman and helps set fire to the bodies. Claudia is angry that Hector has involved her father in his illegal business.

Gael watches on his monitor as teenager Kyle Singer talks to his friend Tim in Canoga Park and admits he was paid to transport cocaine from Tijuana. He is trying to make money as his mother is on dialysis and his father is unemployed.

13:48 President Palmer arrives at the University of Southern California for a debate with Senator John Keeler. It is his first visit to Los Angeles since the attempt on his life. He is met by Wayne, his brother and Chief of Staff.

His private physician, Dr. Anne Packard, arrives and puts a blood pressure cuff onto Palmer's arm over the skin that was affected by the deadly attack three years ago.

Wayne interrupts to inform the President about the virus on the body in Los Angeles and about the Salazar demands.

13:52 Jack clicks a remote control and the windows of his office electronically tint. He rolls up his sleeve and prepares a syringe full of heroin but as he's about to inject his arm, Kim buzzes and asks to speak. Jack throws the syringe across the room in anger.

13:21

14:22

14:00-15:00

Jack cleans up the smashed syringes and finds one vial of heroin that is intact. He puts it into his medical kit. Jack admits using but promises Chase he will now stop.

Chase watches as Kim enters Jack's office to confess they have been dating. Jack doesn't show his concern but he thinks Chase, like himself, won't be able to have a relationship with anyone, because of their job.

Chloe tells Chase she's worried about a possible virus outbreak. Jack and Chase are given transmitters so CTU can track them as they visit Goss's last known address. Jack gets a call from Annicon and he tells the DA that Salazar may be released because of his brother Hector, but won't reveal any more.

14:20 Tony briefs White House Chief of Staff Wayne Palmer on the terrorists' demands. He knows Palmer will not free Salazar, regardless of the threat.

Dr. Macer reports that this virus is engineered to kill ten times faster. She has examined Goss and believes the virus may have been transmitted in crystalline form, in a white powder like cocaine or heroin.

Wayne believes the best thing is to continue with the debate and tells the President he can get his rivals playbook that reveals how he will deal with questions in the debate. Palmer is not interested.

Palmer tells Anne about the virus and she advises him to leave Los Angeles. Wayne warns his brother there are things about Anne that could damage them all.

14:38 A plainclothes officer briefs Jack and Chase about activity inside the condemned building where Goss lived. It is crack den. The CTU agents, who have not fitted their transmitters, go in alone and are stopped by Zach, who had earlier called Kyle and asked him to deliver cocaine at 7.30pm.

Zach is wounded and confesses Goss' supplier is Carlos Corretja from Tijuana. Corretja is one of Salazar's mid-level distributors.

Zach is told to call Corretja after his mule brings in a bag of cocaine. The mule, Kyle, was paid $10,000 even though the cocaine isn't even worth that much. Tony instructs CTU staff to investigate Kyle Singer.

14:59 Hector calls his informant Gael, who says Kyle is at home with the cocaine. Gael is a worker at CTU!

Kyle's girlfriend Linda confronts him about dealing drugs. He says he is making money to keep his family's home. Linda walks out.

95

15:32

15:00-16:00

Jack meets Dr. Nicole Duncan, head of Health Services for Los Angeles, and they join a Hazmat team to visit Singer's house.

Dr. Duncan says Macer's estimates are off. She believes the virus would infect 20% of the population in one week. She spots a heroin vial on the floor of Jack's car.

15:05 Michelle has discovered the terrorist's call was made from inside the United States. Unaware that Gael is the source of the scrambled voice, she asks him to narrow down the area.

At the Salazar ranch, Claudia suggests to Hector he won't stop running the business once Ramon is out of prison. Gael calls to say Jack is on the trail of the virus.

Tony tells his team Kyle may have the virus in what he thinks is a bag of cocaine. Kyle has locked himself in his room after a row with his parents and puts the cocaine into a gym bag.

As he tries to leave, his father grabs the bag. It breaks open and a fan blows powder into the apartment.

15:22 Suddenly a buzz saw cuts through the front door and Kyle's mother dumps the powder into the toilet. Jack, Dr. Duncan and the Hazmat team rush in. Jack tells the Singers that Kyle may have carried a virus from Mexico.

Jack rushes to the biohazard shower, rinses his Hazmat suit, tears the mask off and vomits. Duncan's team discover the powder is harmless.

Jack wonders if Kyle is carrying the virus. The incubation period is fourteen hours, Kyle was in Mexico eleven hours ago and Hector Salazar threatened to release the virus in three hours.

Tony calls to say Annicon is dead. Salazar's guard, whose son had been held hostage, strangled him.

15:35 Kyle calls his girlfriend Linda for help. He needs cash to pay for the cocaine taken by his father. She agrees to steal money from her parents.

Salazar's hired gun, Gomez, is following Kyle. Gael informs him CTU knows the powder does not hold the virus.

Kyle answers his cell phone and his father tells him he may have contracted a virus in Mexico. Kyle hangs up but Tony has already tracked his location to Los Feliz Mall.

Jack drives to the mall with the Hazmat squad. He has blocked Chase from joining his team. Dr. Duncan asks Jack how long he has used heroin as she recognises the symptoms. He admits it was whilst he was undercover with the Salazars.

15:58 Gomez calls Gael to say CTU is about to pick up Kyle. Tony tells Kyle about the virus, unaware that behind him is Gomez with a raised gun. Gomez fires and hits Tony in the neck. Kyle flees. Jack runs to Tony's aid.

16:00-17:00

As Kim and Michelle hear Tony has been shot at the mall there is a second call to CTU demanding Salazar's release.

Those listening are unaware it is Gael's filtered voice. Chloe warns Gael to be sensitive towards Michelle with her husband in hospital. Gael dismisses Chloe with a fake reason when his cell phone rings with a personal call, something that is banned in CTU. The caller to Gael is Hector Salazar who is furious the government has not agreed to release his brother.

16:04

16:05 Gomez follows Kyle in a pickup truck as he makes his way towards Linda's car where he gets behind the steering wheel. Kyle is now unsure that he picked up drugs in Mexico and thinks he may have a disease. Linda wants to get out, but before she can act Gomez and his driver capture her and Kyle and take them to an airproof chamber in a warehouse.

Jack calls to say he will be unable to find Kyle before the virus is due to be released.

16:18 Jack wants to remove Salazar so it looks like a prison break. It would appear Jack had switched sides and it would have to be his last mission and he would be a fugitive from the law.

Jack calls Kim and asks for a prisoner transfer document and claims he is moving Salazar under high security clearance. She tells Jack that Chase went to interrogate Salazar. Chase tells the warden that Salazar is behind a terrorist threat and requests that security cameras are turned off in the cell. He wraps a towel over his right hand and sticks his left fingers into Salazar's throat before punching him demanding to know where Kyle is.

16:50 Jack arrives and knocks Chase unconscious. Stunned Salazar walks out with Jack but is stopped by the warden, who says that transfer access codes have expired. Jack convinces him it is a mistake.

The warden turns the cameras back on and sees Chase, bound and gagged. The alarm sounds and Jack has to force a guard at gunpoint to open up the cells electronically. There is havoc as prisoners are freed in the hallways. Jack and Salazar hide.

16:18

16:54

17:09

17:00-18:00

There's a full riot at the federal holding facility that allows Jack and Salazar to knockout two guards and steal their uniforms. But they are then taken hostage by a group of prisoners. Chase wants Jack and Salazar found and has to reveal the virus threat to the warden.

17:20 Prisoner Peel shoots out a security camera and pulls Jack and another guard from the hostages. He puts a gun on a table and makes them play Russian Roulette. The guard puts the gun to his temple and pulls the trigger. It fires and he falls to the ground.

Salazar is next up against Jack. Salazar says he is a prisoner and Jack confirms he is a federal agent. Jack pulls the trigger. It is empty. Salazar also gets an empty round.

17:29 Kim spots Kyle in a truck on a traffic camera and sees he is being held at gunpoint. Michelle tells Kim that her father had lied about the prison transfer.

An image of the truck is being download when it suddenly stops due to a router error. In the ITS room, Gael is manipulating the router. He tells Kim a line surge may have damaged the router and that he has fixed it. Chloe says a line surge would not have shut down the routers.

Chloe rummages through Jack's office and finds the heroin vial and syringe and shows them to Kim before going to Michelle.

Adam locates the truck carrying Kyle and orders a raid on the warehouse. Inside the warehouse container, Kyle tells Linda the government told his father he wouldn't be contagious for a few more hours. They may survive if they are found in time.

But he breaks into the ceiling and finds wires with which he tries to hang himself. Linda stops him. The SWAT team storm in and shoots the terrorists. They rescue Kyle and Linda.

17:37 Meanwhile, Chase sets explosives on the wall, and Jack notices the light from the agent's headset in the air vent.

As the prisoners chant for the game to continue, Jack shoots Peel in the chest. Suddenly, a blast puts a hole in the wall and Chase leads a raid into the room. Jack and Salazar escape and Chase follows them down a maintenance tunnel with a fibre optic camera on his headset.

Jack makes Salazar take off his guard's uniform. They walk outside and Jack demands the helicopter from Chase. Jack says if he doesn't let Salazar go soon, hundreds of thousands of people will die. They take the chopper and Jack disables the comm and locator.

As workers prepare for Salazar's homecoming in Mexico, Gael phones Hector to say Jack has his brother alive. Hector warns Gael that Kyle must not be captured.

17:44 In the televised debate, Senator Keeler claims Palmer's current girlfriend, Anne, fabricated results of a clinical drug trial that later caused three deaths. Palmer says the accusation is false, although he has already secretly agreed to pay cash to her ex-husband, Ted, who has blackmailed him. The President phones Wayne and calls off the deal.

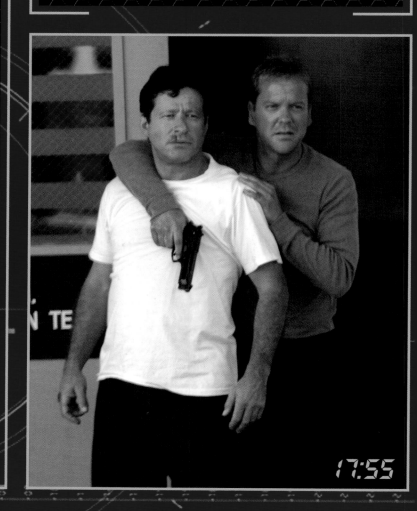

17:55

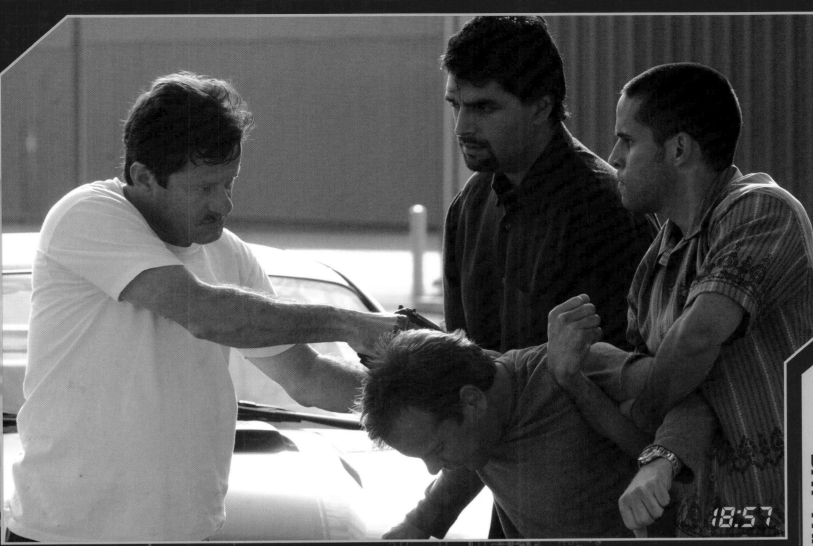

18:57

18:00-19:00

Jack flies the chopper towards downtown Los Angeles, knowing he can't be shot down over a populated area. District Director Ryan Chappelle assumes control of CTU and instructs Major Blanchard to shoot Jack down before he reaches downtown. Chappelle informs CTU staff that as the virus is contained Jack and Salazar are expendable. He doesn't need White House authorisation to attack as Jack is a fugitive. Chase warns him that Jack and the President are close and Chappelle holds back on firing.

18:10 The President is updated about what is happening through his transmitter earwig. He stops the debate saying there is a national security emergency.

Palmer goes backstage and tells Wayne he cannot order Jack's death. Wayne wonders if ridding the world of Salazar is more important. The President authorises Chappelle to give the order to fire.

18:24 CTU falls silent as the military pilots lock on the chopper's position. Jack flies between tall buildings and the military have to stand down. Chappelle gets ground units ready to bring Jack in as the helicopter lands in a downtown street. Salazar and Jack dash into a Metro Station. Kim tells Chase there is only one emergency exit, a block away in an alley. Chase finds an open grate at the exit and has the area sealed. Jack and Salazar take a set of keys from a valet stand and steal a car.

Jack calls Hector Salazar's pilot in a private jet. Gael listens in and buffers the call so CTU can't track it. The pilot arranges to meet at the Santa Margarita airstrip.

In the IT room, Gael talks to the pilot as he watches the private jet land. Jack pulls up next to the plane but is knocked out by Salazar's henchman and taken onboard.

Back at CTU, Kim notices Gael did not log off and she sees a video feed of Jack being carried onto a plane. Gael returns before she is able to call anyone. He pulls a gun.

In Mexico, Claudia tells Hector it is dangerous to allow Jack to bring Ramon to the ranch.

18:30 Kyle and Linda are taken to the National Health Services Center. As his parents worry that he has hours to live, Dr. Duncan reveals tests prove Kyle is not affected with the virus. She informs Chappelle who is puzzled.

19:00-20:00

Gael tapes Kim to a chair and covers her mouth with duct tape, before deleting all evidence of Salazar off his computer.

Before visiting Tony who is recovering in hospital, Michelle puts Gael in charge. Gael watches Kim on a hand-held monitor as he leaves for a briefing.

Gael tells Adam that Kim has been given a new task by Chappelle and can't make the meeting. But then he watches on his monitor as Adam is unable to get into the IT room. Gael denies changing the access code. As Michelle overrides the code, Gael disappears.

19:11 Adam finds Kim tied up and she reveals Gael was responsible. Security arrest Gael trying to escape but he refuses to talk under interrogation.

When Gael's phone rings Adam and Kim start to track the call. Gael answers and tells Hector his brother is safely on his way. The call is not long enough to be traced.

Chappelle briefs his staff about Kyle being virus-free and makes finding Jack and Salazar a priority. He knows Jack has been using heroin, and believes Chase has been covering for him.

Chase questions Salazar's accountant about Hector's whereabouts. The man discovers deposits made to an account in Las Nieves. Chase orders the accountant to

prepare his private plane and then calls Kim to say he is going to Mexico to find Jack.

19:24 Handcuffed aboard the jet, Jack tries to persuade henchman Pedro to help him as he saved Salazar. Jack starts to convulse and as Pedro comes over Jack kicks him and chokes him with his legs. He grabs his guard's gun and handcuff keys. As Salazar enters the cabin, Jack grabs his arm and holds him at gunpoint.

19:31 The Presidential cavalcade arrives at District headquarters. White House Press Secretary Gerry Whitehorn tells Palmer Anne will hurt his public standing. Wayne agrees. Anne gets a call from her ex-husband, Ted, who claims he has papers that will prove her innocence

19:43 Michelle goes to the hospital and explains to Tony how Jack broke Salazar out of prison. She reveals that Gael is mole.

The couple return to CTU and Tony stops Gael's interrogation. He orders Chappelle out of the room.

Salazar's plane lands. Hector embraces his brother and then Jack, who he says did a good job. They both have the same tattoo on their arms. Ramon is confused.

Jack presses a button on his watch. In the interrogation room at CTU, Gael's hand-held beeps. Tony reveals he and Gael have been working to infiltrate Jack back in with the Salazars.

20:00 – 21:00

Chappelle is angry to hear from Tony that Jack is back undercover with the Salazars.

Tony informs the President that all of the events from the infected body to the prison break were an elaborate sting. Jack has gone undercover to find a group of Ukrainian scientists who are trying to sell a weaponised virus. Jack has suggested the Salazars as buyers and has set up a meeting between the two sides in Mexico.

Jack asks Palmer in a pre-recorded video message to give Tony the power to work with the military to grab the virus.

Tony shows CTU staff that Jack's transponder puts him at a ranch in Mexico. Kim reveals to Tony that Chase has tracked Jack to Las Nieves.

20:07 At the ranch in Las Nieves, Hector explains to Ramon how Jack offered an opportunity to make billions. By purchasing a deadly virus from Ukrainian scientists, they can sell it on to Al-Qaeda and North Korea.

Jack will buy the virus within the hour and make $50 million. He sees it as compensation for losing his wife, bringing down Salazar and then being demoted at CTU.

Ramon thinks Hector is crazy for trusting Jack. But he says their contacts in the American agencies and military confirm Jack is a fugitive. He adds that he will kill Jack when they have the virus.

As Jack waits, Claudia approaches him and says she feels betrayed - she learned he was undercover last time he was with the Salazars and he had promised to help her escape.

20:10

20:20

20:20 Tony, who is in a very weakened state, sends agent Rafael Gutierrez to find Chase. Gutierrez finds the accountant's empty plane in the desert and is then held at gunpoint by Chase who check his credentials.

Chase calls Tony but a sniper fells Gutierrez. Chase drives off as Tony, Michelle and Kim hear gunshots and then a car crash. Chase is taken prisoner.

20:22 Anne arrives at her ex-husband Ted's office and notices he has a gun. Before she can grab the firearm he shoots himself. Anne informs Palmer about the suicide and letters clearing her.

Wayne examines the papers from Ted and says they will clear her name. But Anne ends her relationship with Palmer saying she is unable to live this type of life.

20:55 Jack uses a satellite phone to call Michael Amador, his Ukrainian contact. Henchmen arrive at the ranch house with Chase who Salazar recognises as Jack's partner.

Jack confirms to Chase he is with the Salazars, raises his gun to his partner's head and fires. The chamber is empty. They all head to a safe house to await Amador's return call.

Jack notices his watch isn't working. Gael reports to Tony that the transponder on Jack's watch went dead.

21:04

21:43 At the ranch, Claudio manages to get rid of Chase's guard and tells him about Jack's mission. She says she will think of a way to save him.

Claudia tells her younger brother, Sergio, to be ready to leave and grabs a knife from the kitchen.

21:47 President Palmer insists to the press he ended the televised debate because of a national security threat. He assures them the public is safe.

Wayne tells Palmer that CTU have lost trace on Jack. The President is called by Alan Milliken, a wealthy campaign contributor, who asks to see Palmer alone.

Palmer learns Milliken's wife had an affair with Wayne when he worked for the financier. Wayne offers to resign but Palmer refuses his offer.

21:22

21:00–22:00

Salazar's convoy of trucks halts at an abandoned farmhouse and Hector notices Jack is suffering withdrawal. He hands him some pills. Jack confronts Claudia in private and confesses his mission. He needs a cell phone and to keep Chase alive.

21:17 Back at CTU, Kim asks Tony for a format code. He tells her the old code before realising his mistake. Kim reveals the mistake to Michelle who tells Chappelle she believes Tony is not up to the job. Chappelle tests Tony but allows him to continue working.

21:22 At the meeting spot Amador greets Jack, who introduces the Salazars. Amador reveals there is a rival bidder for the virus – Nina Myers, who pulls up in a second car. She sees Jack and orders her men to kill him. Jack claims he quit CTU. Amador assures everyone the area is secure. The Salazars bid $200 million. But Nina offers $240 million.

21:36

22:00-23:00

Gael gets a call from Hector revealing Nina has the virus. Gael is given Amador's cell phone number by Jack and when their location is tracked, Tony orders CTU commandos to move in. Tony tells Chappelle that Jack may ask Nina, who had been exiled to North Africa, to help him retrieve the virus.

Jack and the Salazars return to the farmhouse where Sergio tells Hector his sister plans to take them away. Claudia claims she was trying to scare Sergio as he was misbehaving.

Hector asks Chase if he has back up and when he refuses to answer, shoots him in his left hand.

As Jack and Ramon leave to track down Nina to retrieve the virus, Claudia tells her father to sabotage all of the trucks except one so they can't be followed.

She goes to Eduardo, who is guarding Chase, and says Hector wants her to interrogate the prisoner. But she hands a knife to the agent and throws gasoline on to the guard. Chase stabs the man. Claudia, her father, Sergio and Chase drive off in a truck as Hector fires at them. Claudia is shot in the head. The truck breaks down and Chase calls Tony to ask for a chopper.

22:20 Gael calls Jack to say Amador is at an abandoned church. Jack and Salazar arrive with their headlights off and spot Nina with Amador. Jack goes in alone but hands Salazar night-vision goggles so he can watch.

Jack climbs up to a window and hears Amador tell Nina he will call with the location of the virus. But Jack is spotted and shots are fired. Nina tries to leave but Jack stops her at gunpoint.

Salazar watches as Jack takes Nina into the church. He offers her ten times what she has paid if she gives the virus to the Salazars. Nina believes Jack is still working for CTU.

But Jack claims Kim blames him for her mother's death and he wants the money to help rebuild her life. He says he is unable to return home following the illegal prison break.

Nina raises her gun to Jack's forehead but then turns around and shoots the guard. She asks if he can forgive her for killing his wife, Teri. Jack says if he wanted revenge, she would already be dead. She ties him to a chair.

22:28 Wayne tells the President that three Senators will not support the White House's health care bill as Milliken got them to change their votes. The President vows revenge.

Wayne goes to a darkened cocktail lounge, to see Milliken's wife, Julia. He asks for help in getting her husband off the President's back. Julia wants Wayne to become her lover again. Wayne says no, and she refuses to help.

Wayne reports back to the President who calls his ex-wife Sherry and asks for help.

22:40 Chloe gets an urgent phone call from a girl called Sarah who she agrees to meet outside CTU. The teenager has a baby in her car which Chloe takes into the office. Chappelle finds the baby hidden under Chloe's desk and she claims her babysitter let her down.

23:00-00:00

Nina is caught off guard as Jack head butts her. He then smashes into the wall to break the wooden chair he's chained to and holds a piece of wood to Nina's neck.

Jack says he is a fugitive and she is the only one Amador will sell the virus to. He promises she will get her $20 million fee.

23:06 Back at CTU, Adam finds Amador's location but it cannot be identified from the satellite. Kim discovers Nina is involved.

The chopper lands and picks up Chase, Claudia's father and brother shortly before Hector arrives and finds Claudia's body.

Hector phones Gael, who traces the call, and says Chase has escaped. Gael claims the CTU don't know where Chase is. Hector calls his brother to call off the deal but he says they must deliver the virus to their buyer as promised.

Salazar enters the church as Jack checks Nina's laptop. He claims Nina has agreed the exchange and they are awaiting Amador's call.

23:24 Chase wants to track Amador as his partner's life is at stake.

Chappelle tells the Delta team to stand off until they have visual of the virus.

Amador collects a briefcase from his couriers. It contains a steel cylinder containing a vial of white crystalline powder immersed in a green liquid.

Nina whispers to Salazar that Jack is working with CTU to set him up. He doesn't believe her. Amador calls to confirm Nina's bank account. When he sees the money is there, Amador arranges a meeting place.

Amador calls someone to say he will hand over the virus within the hour. Adam tracks Amador heading east and Gael suggests intercepting him. Tony wants a signal from Jack.

Hector joins his brother, Nina and Jack. Jack secretly dials Michelle on his cell so she can listen in. He says they are meeting Amador. Tony agrees to send in the Delta teams.

Captain Reiss mobilises his men but says he will send in just one observer. Chase volunteers and pulls on camouflage gear.

The Salazar brothers argue over whether the deal should go ahead and Ramon shoots Hector in the back.

23:43 The President insists to Milliken that he will not fire his brother. Palmer tells Wayne that Sherry will sort the problem so they can focus on the virus threat.

Sherry thanks Palmer for keeping her out of prison and vows to help him. Palmer explains the Milliken situation and Sherry admits to knowing one skeleton in the Senator's closet. Wayne asks Sherry to claim she can't find anything with which to blackmail, so the President will accept his own resignation.

23:55 Chloe asks Kim to watch her baby while she goes to a briefing. As Michelle and Tony brief Chappelle they hear a baby cry. Chappelle wants to suspend Chloe, but Michelle says they need her to take care of the digitally enhanced audio surveillance from Mexico.

00:00-01:00

Hector, shot in the back, is still alive, but it is too risky to take him to hospital. Ramon shoots him again and kills him before he, Nina and Jack go to meet Amador at Posta Mita.

In the woods at Posta Mita, Chase sets up a parabolic dish to pick up sound. Chloe will be his link at CTU.

Jack and Salazar arrive and Ramon has his men hide. Nina tells Salazar she is sure a CTU reconnaissance man will be watching. Salazar sends two guards to check. Chase spots the two men.

Salazar enters the meeting place and radios the two men. One, Pablo, responds saying no one is there. He is unaware Chase has Pablo at knifepoint. Chase knocks Pablo out.

Salazar removes Nina's handcuffs and sends her to meet Amador. Chase watches Nina leave the building and radios CTU. Tony orders in the Delta teams.

Tony gets an urgent call from Kim who says Chloe claimed the baby belongs to her boyfriend, Eric, who is trying to hide it from his ex-wife, who is abusing the child. But she has discovered no abuse charges filed with Child Protective Services.

Tony needs Chloe as she is the only person who can filter the audio streams from Chase. He says he will deal with the problem once they have the virus.

00:33 Chase reports to CTU that Amador and his men have arrived. Nina tells Amador she will transfer funds once she verifies the virus. He removes a canister from the case and hands over the vial. She puts the vial into a spectroscope and it confirms the virus.

Amador takes back the vial from Nina, and puts something in his breast pocket. She arranges the transfer. Amador gives Nina the briefcase and leaves.

Static interrupts Chase's broadcast and CTU can't hear him. Chloe explains she changed dishes during the operation. Chase comes back on line.

Jack and Salazar see Nina returning. Salazar takes the vial and aims a gun on Jack. Salazar says Jack caused his brother's death. Before he can fire, Chase shoots Salazar in the shoulder.

00:54

00:21

As the guards return fire, Nina runs into the woods. Jack grabs a weapon from a guard and begins taking out the others. Chase tells Tony the Delta team has arrived.

00:51 Sherry meets a man named Kevin Kelly in a run-down mobile home. He admits he saw Milliken driving a car that killed his daughter and took money to keep his mouth shut. He agrees to confess if the President pardons his son who is in jail for murder.

Wayne warns Palmer that Sherry will have her own agenda and says he would rather resign than agree to her request.

When Sherry returns to the trailer Kelly has gone and the place is ransacked. Sherry calls Milliken's wife, Julia, and offers her a way of escaping her husband.

Wayne calls Tony and says the Pentagon is furious they weren't told about the secret mission. The President will hold Tony, Jack and Gael accountable.

00:53 Jack is relieved Chase is all right and they follow Salazar, who they find with gunshot wounds. He is about to hand over the virus cylinder when a timer buzzes. The cylinder explodes.

Amador had switched vials.

Captain Reiss stops Amador's truck at gunpoint but his soldiers are taken out by snipers in the trees. Amador smashes his cell phone and drives away. Adam loses Amador's cell phone signal.

Tony tells Jack that Amador cannot be tracked as there is no satellite coverage of the area.

01:19

murder. If Milliken goes to prison, Julia will get everything. Sherry needs Milliken's cell phone and sneaks into the bedroom to take it. She gives the last dialled calls to someone over the phone so they can be tracked. Milliken enters the room and Sherry confronts him about Kelly's daughter's death.

Milliken stumbles out of his wheelchair as he fights with Sherry. As he gasps for air Sherry stops Julia from handing over his pills. They watch as he dies.

Sherry instructs Julia to call 911 after an hour and pretend she found her husband's body.

01:56 As the plane begins to rise, the pilot tells Jack he has orders from Tony to return to Mexico. Jack is about to force him to land at L.A. when they hear Chloe has cracked the code.

Chloe is shocked when she sees the baby being taken by Child Protective Services and reveals the father is Chase.

01:00–02:00

As Nina corners Chase in the woods, Jack arrives and captures her. The two agents take her on a Navy plane from Las Nieves to Los Angeles. Nina reveals that Amador always deals with a man named Alvers on the west coast but she has no idea who he is.

01:21 CTU techie Dalton Furelle discovers Amador and Alvers were once suspected of manufacturing weapons-grade Anthrax. Tony assigns Michelle to help Dalton trace Alvers. Nina reveals a Felco prefix number that gives an internet socket where she says Alvers can be reached.

Jack dials the socket and CTU systems immediately lock up and computers crash as a self-propagating code leaks into their database. Nina says the call triggered a worm.

Jack suggests Chloe is given the task of saving the network. But Chappell has put Chloe under guard as she won't speak about the baby.

Nina wants the plane to return to Mexico before she will stop the worm. Chappelle relents and allows Chloe to examine the virus threat. Jack shows Nina on a laptop how the worm will bring down the CTU network in a few minutes. She tells Chloe how to slow the worm for 20 minutes.

Wayne reports to Palmer that Amador, a known arms dealer, has escaped in Mexico with the virus. Sherry calls to say Kelly has gone missing and that she suspects Milliken. As Sherry arrives to see Julia Milliken she tells her to disable the security cameras.

01:33 Sherry suggests Julia helps her to prove Milliken was involved in the car crash and possibly Kelly's

01:42

01:45

02:00-03:00

As the plane lands, Chloe calls Chase to say everyone at CTU knows about his daughter. Chase explains to Kim he only recently discovered he was a father from an ex-girlfriend who did not want the child. Chloe has been helping take care of the child.

Nina is taken to an interrogation room at CTU as Jack is ushered to a clinic to have his drug problem checked. On the way he quickly speaks to Kim and says he didn't tell her about the heroin as he didn't want to worry her.

Michelle and Dalton prepare the interrogation monitors and Tony tells them to focus on Nina's eyes. They may be able to pick something up by her eye movements. Nina tries to unsettle Tony during questioning by bringing up their past relationship. She claims not to know Alvers but her pulse spikes when it is mentioned he was tested for HIV.

But Tony makes little more headway and sends for the torture specialist. The specialist applies a needle to the back of Nina's neck but it hits an artery. Tony applies pressure to the wound and Michelle calls for medical assistance.

Nina is rushed to the CTU clinic but as doctors work she squeezes shut the drip tube delivering anaesthetic, shuts her eyes and pretends to pass out. Tony leaves to tell Jack and Chappelle what is happening.

Meanwhile, Jack is speaking to an investigator from the Inspector General's office. The investigator, Plachecki, asks about his heroin addiction and his six weeks of use

before he entered Salazar's gang. Jack says he had to be prepared. Chappelle suggests Plachecki records that Jack did not use drugs until the first meeting with Salazar. Jack refuses to lie.

Suddenly, an alarm sounds. The clinic's doctors and medics are found dead and Nina had disappeared.

02:21 Amador enters a seedy bar carrying a briefcase and meets Alvers, who asks about Nina. He is relieved when Amador says she is probably dead. Amador hands over the container and Alvers calls someone to say he has the virus.

02:52 Wayne warns the President the virus may already be in Los Angeles. Palmer asks for two containment strategies, covert and public, within thirty minutes.

Wayne then tells Palmer that Milliken is dead. Sherry admits she went to the Milliken estate and after a row the Senator suffered a heart attack. Wayne leaves Palmer's office and calls Julia who says Sherry stopped her from giving Milliken his medication.

02:57 Kim runs into a stairwell and takes a gun from a dead guard. She discovers Nina in CTU control room, ripping out wires. Nina warns Kim to walk away and slowly raises her gun hand. Suddenly, Nina is shot in the shoulder by Jack, from behind Kim. Nina's hand moves closer to the gun on the ground but Jack fires three shots into her.

03:04

03:56

03:00-04:00

Chappelle enters the transformer room where Nina's body lies dead on the ground and angrily questions Jack. Video surveillance would confirm if he was only defending himself. Kim didn't witness the shooting as her father made her leave the room.

Tony informs his staff that Jack killed Nina as she tried to escape. He reveals new information about detonating devices stolen from Russia that could be used with the virus.

Chloe discovers one of Amador's bank accounts was activated from a local server just a few minutes ago.

Chappelle accuses Jack of standing in front of the security camera as he shot Nina but their discussion is interrupted by the lead on Amador. Jack and Chase convince Chappelle that Jack is needed and Chappelle reluctantly agrees.

03:04 In the nightclub, Amador allows Saunders to takes the vials of virus. Amador asks why he chose a limited target and Saunders says he only wants to send a message.

Saunders is not happy with Amador for trusting Jack and accuses him of being greedy. He hands Amador and Alvers half of the $200 million they were due and says they will receive the balance after they hit the hotel with the virus.

Alvers arrives at the Chandler Plaza Hotel by taxi with a briefcase in his hand. He enters the lobby and calls Amador to say he needs 25 minutes.

03:15 Wayne advises the President to stay away from Milliken's death. Wayne confronts Sherry and says he knows she prevented Milliken taking his medication.

Detective Norris tells Julia that her maid heard a car and thought she saw a light-coloured Mercedes. He asks why the security system was shut down an hour before Milliken's death. Julia denies any knowledge.

Norris phones Sherry to say Julia claims she was with her. Sherry claims Julia is lying as she was with Palmer all night. The detective says Julia accused Sherry of helping her withhold medication.

03:33 Jack and Chase arrive at the nightclub where Chloe tracked Amador's transaction. Jack and Chase lead a SWAT raid and Jack pins Amador to the ground.

Amador refuses to talk. Jack has Chase slice Amador's palm with a knife. He passes out. Jack orders Chase to repeat the action when Amador wakes up.

Jack tells Tony and Chappelle the virus has been passed on and that Amador suggested whoever is behind this knows him very well.

Amador's laptop has the full schematics of the Chandler Hotel. Tony orders an NHS team to the hotel and notifies Phillips, the hotel's head of security, that a toxic substance may have been released in the building.

Chappelle asks Tony to control information flow at the office, and sends Michelle to lead the on-site team. Tony orders her to stay out of the hotel until NHS arrive with biohazard suits. She hangs up annoyed.

Gael finds an image of Alvers on the hotel's security camera. Against orders Michelle, Gael and others enter the building.

Phillips says that they may have spotted Alvers dressed as a maintenance man. His assistant is checking him out.

Alvers enters the ventilation room, takes out the detonator and inserts a virus-filled vial. He places it below a fan that blows air into the building.

Michelle finds Phillips' assistant dead and spots Alvers. He runs but she takes him down and handcuffs him to a pipe. Alvers admits the virus has been released.

Gael finds the detonator and opens the fan unit, but the detonator explodes and a fine, white powder sprays into his face and into the air conditioning shaft.

03:56 Chaos ensues when a number of the hotel guests begin getting nosebleeds. One of the irate people throws a trashcan at the front door and smashes the glass. Michelle fires her gun into the air to make the man move away from the window. She threatens to shoot him if he tries to leave. As the man makes his way out, Michelle fires two shots into his back. The other guests are shocked.

04:00-05:00

Michelle learns from Alvers that there are eleven more vials of the virus. He does not know their locations.

Tony briefs Dr. Nicole Duncan as she heads to the hotel. Chappelle tells Tony no one is to leave the hotel and anyone attempting to escape will be shot dead. Cell phone signals are jammed so no one can make contact to the outside.

Chappelle calls Jack with the information and he handcuffs Amador to a rusty pipe. He manages to loosen the pipe and escape. But Kim is monitoring a transponder Jack has placed in the bandage on Amador hand. She calls Jack and he and Chase follow.

The pair hope Amador will need his boss to help him escape. Amador calls his employer, Stephen Saunders, who instructs him to ensure he is not followed. Saunders hands a henchman a cell phone and tells him to release the vial of virus when the phone rings twice.

He gives Amador an address not knowing Jack is following with back-up on the way.

04:23 The virus has contaminated the entire hotel and Gael begins to show symptoms when his nose bleeds. Michelle asks Alvers to tell her what he did to alter the virus, which is meant to have a 14-hour incubation period.

Hotel bellhop Margolis, who has been asked to stay on after his shift, is annoyed that his boss wont tell him what is happening and goes in search of an exit.

Margolis sees Gael, overhears his conversation, with Michelle about the virus and sets off a fire alarm. He grabs a set of keys and a gun from a drawer. Michelle orders the agents and hotel workers to prevent people exiting and to tell everyone it was a false alarm.

Phillips alerts Michelle a fire door has been opened on the west side of the hotel. She find Margolis trying to unlock a door and he pulls a gun. Michelle has to confess the truth and says he will be

responsible for spreading the disease if he leaves. He hands over the gun.

A number of the hotel guests get nosebleeds. There is panic and Michelle is forced to fire two shots into the back of a man who tries to flee.

04:50 Palmer orders Wayne to notify the California governor of the virus at the Chandler Hotel.

Sherry tells Palmer that Julia had told police about her involvement in Milliken's death. Sherry has told the police she was with her ex-husband at the time. Wayne warns Palmer that Sherry will be arrested unless he backs up her alibi. Palmer refuses to lie.

The Los Angeles Chief of Police arrives to see Palmer and the President and says Sherry was with him when Milliken died. He is not happy about lying for her.

04:54 Jack and Chase watch Amador take a briefcase from a man inside a car. The car explodes. As Jack rushes to the wreckage his cell phone rings. Saunders wants to speak to the President.

Saunders tells Palmer he will release the virus and kill most of the American population unless his demands are met. He says he will call back.

`05:07`

05:00-06:00

A SWAT team surrounds the hotel as Michelle orders guests to stay calm She is again forced to fire her gun into the air to keep order. Guests return to their rooms.

Phillips asks if everyone in the hotel will die but Michelle believes some will be immune. Tony assures Michelle she was right to shoot the man who tried to leave.

Michelle quizzes Alvers about who hired him. He describes a man he met in Chinatown. His information is used to pull up mugshots of people involved in cases dealt with by Jack and Alvers recognises one of the pictures.

It is Stephen Saunders, a British agent loaned to CTU from MI6 for the operation against Victor Drazen in Kosovo. It was believed Saunders was dead. Jack thinks he might have been captured and has spent the last ten years in a foreign prison.

He calls Trevor Tomlinson at MI6 who gives the name of Diana White, a woman who ran an escort service and lived with Saunders. She is now in Los Angeles.

`05:28` Chase pulls up information on White. He believes Saunders may have blackmailed her clients to raise money for his operation. Jack and Chase break into White's house.

She says Saunders left her.

White is taken to MI6 where Tomlinson reveals Diana is the owner of the address in Chinatown where Saunders was last seen. A helicopter rises to the window and machine gun fire kills Diana. Tomlinson is hit but tells Jack the number of the server where the Saunders files are stored.

Jack and Chase run downstairs, killing two gunmen, and find four dead bodies in the computer room. There is a bomb attached to the computer mainframe. Jack pulls out the hard drive and escapes as the bomb explodes.

One of Saunders's men reports Jack's escape but says the hard drive was destroyed. Saunders, who ordered Diana's death, hears Chappelle has been investigating his Cayman bank accounts.

`05:39` Tony tells Kim that NHS reckon there is a 100% mortality rate from the virus. Chappelle advises Tony to assume the worst for Michelle and asks him to track bank accounts from Amador's computer to find a link to Saunders.

Michelle speaks to Gael in isolation and is shocked at the boils on his face and his bloodstained shirt. When Gael dies,

Michelle asks if the infected hotel guests can have suicide capsules.

`05:44` The President meets Homeland Security Chief, Joseph O'Laughlin, and issues orders for airlines to be warned of a possible nationwide grounding.

Saunders calls and demands the Secret Service pick up a package from a mailbox within ten minutes. Agent Pierce collects the package that contains a cell phone with a sub-channel chip so it cannot be traced.

Saunders calls on the phone and tells the President to call a press conference. Palmer must use the phrase "the sky is falling" during the briefing.

As they approach the press briefing, Wayne tells the President the FBI is ready if the phrase "the sky is falling" triggers suspicious activity. Palmer announces the threat level has been elevated to red and that airports will be closed. He says the phrase.

Wayne briefs the President on the MI6 attack and Palmer wonders if he triggered it. Saunders calls Palmer and wants Chappelle killed. His body is to be delivered to the downtown train yard by 7am. Palmer refuses, and Saunders says the Chandler Hotel incident will be repeated elsewhere if he does not comply.

`05:45`

06:00-07:00

As Jack returns to CTU with the hard drive the President who reveals Saunders wants Chappelle's body delivered to the train yard calls him. Jack is puzzled. He orders Chloe to bring the search for Saunders back to CTU from District without telling Chappelle.

06:15 Tony and Jack downgrade Chappelle's security clearance but keep the move quiet.

Chappelle asks Jack what Palmer called for and is told the truth. Jack says will try to capture Saunders before the hour is up. Chappelle is unable to search Saunders's offshore bank account as it's encrypted. He wonders if he is the target because of something he has discovered.

As a helicopter stands by to take Chappelle to the train yard, Chloe manages to decrypt the bank account. Saunders made a transfer from an address in downtown LA forty-five minutes ago. Tony sends Chase to raid the apartment. Jack takes Chappelle to the waiting helicopter.

Chase and another agent spot three guards as they arrive at the address. They shoot the guards and enter the building. Another strike team uses the fire escape to reach the roof. The apartment is empty, except for a switching mode that has been relaying calls.

Saunders calls Jack's cell phone and says to leave Chappelle's body in a van at the train yard. Jack calls CTU and asks for satellite imagery to track the van. He then takes Chappelle into the yard and reluctantly fires point blank at Chappelle's head.

06:17 Suicide capsules are delivered to Michelle at the hotel. She admits to the guests that there is no chance of recovery once symptoms have appeared and the estimated time of death is six hours.

Michelle warns Tony that a man has slipped out of the hotel. Fingerprints are taken from a belt belonging to a woman he was with in a bid to find out who he is. They come up with 300 potential matches from a partial print. The woman who spent the night with the man identifies him from mugshots.

Elsewhere in town, William Cole slips into his house and awakens his wife to say he worked late. In the bathroom Cole notices blood dripping from his nose.

06:41 Gerry Whitehorn, Palmer's press secretary, says a reporter from the Los Angeles Times is asking if a toxic accident at the Chandler Hotel is connected to the White House's red alert. Wayne tells Whitehorn the truth but Palmer says he must not go public.

All flights from LAX have been grounded and Saunders learns only three of his couriers have reached other American cities. He revises his casualties to five million

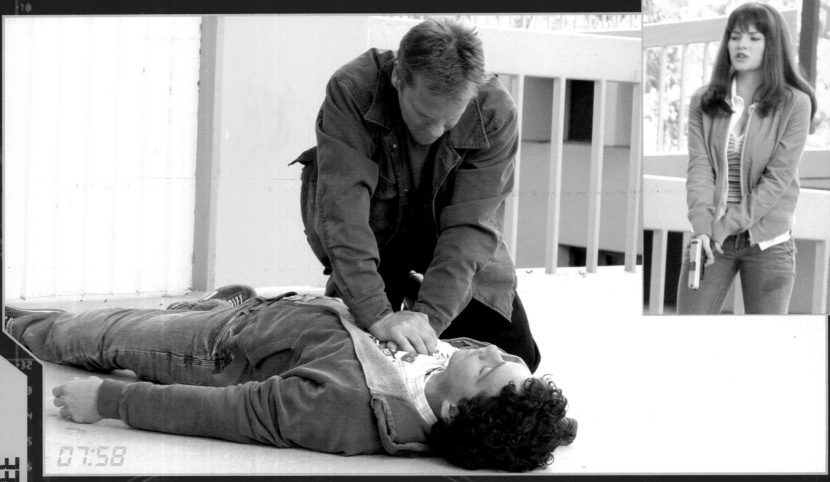

07:58

07:00-08:00

Jack backs away from Chappelle's body as masked men approach from a black van. They check the body for trackers and warn Jack against following them.

Jack calls Wayne Palmer with an update. The President is adamant he will not yield to any more of Saunders's demands. Jack believes Saunders will release more virus.

Kim, Chloe and Adam discover Saunders has a daughter in Santa Barbara. Jack suggests they substitute Jane Saunders with a look-alike agent. Kim is the closest match and agrees to the mission. Jack orders his daughter not to go but she insists. He hands her a gun as they leave in a chopper.

07:27 Palmer tells his Cabinet via video monitors that the virus has been released at the Chandler Hotel. He had to give in to Saunders's demand and kill Chappelle. Palmer says he is more concerned with saving millions of lives than about his own re-election.

Saunders calls the President and demands a list of all foreign nationals working as spies across the globe. If he doesn't receive the list within one hour, Saunders will release two more vials of the virus.

07:32 Michelle does not yet know if she has contracted the virus. Chase arrives at the home of Cole, the man who left the hotel, and finds a bloody tissue.

Cole visits a drug store before heading for an emergency room. A nurse recognises him from a news report and Chase heads to the medical center.

Tony works out how many people Cole could have come in contact with. A few pharmacy customers are not identified, and some patients left the E.R. before quarantine was in place. There could be 75 people infected.

07:41 Jane Saunders gets in her car and heads to work at the University of California as her father's henchmen keep watch.

Jack and Kim are met in Santa Barbara by Agent Forrester. He has set up surveillance cameras to watch Jane work at the reference desk in the campus library.

An agent purposely spills a drink on Jane's pants. When she goes to the restroom, another agent chloroforms Jane and Kim puts on her clothes. Jack warns Kim through her earwig that Saunders's man is in a red shirt. Jane Saunders refuses to help Jack contact her father.

Forrester loses Kim on the camera. A young guy approaches Kim, pulls out a gun and threatens to kill her if she doesn't say where Jane Saunders is. He drags Kim out of the library and as they struggle she pulls out her gun and shoots him.

08:00-09:00

Two new potential virus victims are discovered in the city as Jack tries to convince Jane Saunders that her father is a terrorist.

08:07 Jack shows Jane photos from his mission in Kosovo with Saunders. The U.S. and British governments thought Saunders died. Jack then shows photos of Saunders with arms dealers and biological weapons manufacturers.

He plays an audio file of Saunders threatening the President about releasing the virus. Jane is shown the people at the Chandler Plaza Hotel who are suffering. She gives Jack a phone number she has for emergencies. Jack tells Jane that she must contact her father and keep him on the line so the call can be traced.

Saunders answers the call from Jane but a henchman sees it is being monitored. Adam and Chloe trace the call and Tony sends Chase's team to the location as Jack heads there in the chopper.

Via satellite, Adam tracks anyone coming in or out of Saunders's building. Saunders is aware he has been discovered but believes he has a better chance of escape with more agents around. Saunders shoots a henchman who tries to leave.

08:27 Tests show Michelle has immunity to the virus. Tony is overcome with emotion as they both escaped death today.

Michelle is loaded into a van with the immune guests. One of the victims who tested positive is Adam's sister.

08:45

08:32

08:45 Snipers are already in place when Jack and Chase arrive at the building. Jack hails Saunders on a bullhorn and says the President will no longer give in to his demands.

He says Saunders must surrender as his daughter is being held hostage. Saunders calls Jack and says he needs a few minutes to think.

Saunders takes a call with news that a task has been completed. He then phones Tony at CTU and gives him a web socket number. Tony opens the socket and sees video of Michelle in the back of a van. Saunders warns Michelle will be dead in fifteen seconds if Tony doesn't order the teams on site to the front entrance.

When Tony won't agree he sees a knife come up to Michelle's face on the video. Tony relents and radios the team leader. When Saunders sees the snipers move off he walks out the back entrance unnoticed.

09:00-10:00

When Saunders doesn't emerge, Jack orders the apartment to be gassed. He is shocked Tony moved the teams to the front of the building.

Tony deletes satellite imagery of Saunders leaving the building. Saunders calls Tony on his cell phone and threatens to kill Michelle if his daughter is not released. The President is adamant Jane Saunders is held.

Going through the satellite footage, Chloe notices some frames are missing. She suspects Saunders has a mole inside CTU.

09:19 Saunders calls Tony and asks to speak to his daughter. He lets Michelle briefly talk to Tony then Jane is put on speakerphone. Saunders tells her he is only doing things for a "good cause." Tony gives Chloe a record of Saunders's call but doesn't want her to tell Adam.

Chloe gets a call from Dr. Macer who says the agent assigned to Michelle is not answering his phone. She tells Tony that Michelle is missing. Tony claims he secretly moved Michelle.

Adam, who confirms the missing satellite frames, warns Tony that security has been breached. He orders a lock down.

Jack interrogates Tony about their being a mole inside CTU. Jack offers to call Brad Hammond at Division, but Tony says he already has a conference call scheduled. However, Adam tells Jack no conference call is booked with Hammond.

09:28 Senator Keeler asks his chief of staff to use contacts at the Pentagon to find out what is really going on. He gets a surprise call from Sherry Palmer who has a proposition. She explains she was an accessory to the murder of Alan Milliken, and that Palmer lied to the police. Sherry has the prescription bottle Milliken was reaching for when he suffered a heart attack. Palmer will drop out of the campaign race if Keeler blackmails him for the evidence. In return Sherry wants a job on Keeler's White House staff.

Wayne informs Palmer he has heard Sherry met privately with Keeler. Palmer insists they focus on the virus threat.

09:31 Jack accuses Tony of lying and Tony admits he made a mistake and wiped the frames. Jack says he is taking away his command of CTU.

Tony calls Saunders in a panic with news that Jack is now in charge. Saunders says to get Jane out of the building or Michelle will be killed. Jack wants Kim to monitor and flag communications. He doesn't know who else to trust.

Tony sees Jack calling Adam, and turns on the audio feed at Adam's desk. Jack asks Adam to send Chloe to his office. Tony calls Adam and offers to tell Chloe that Jack wants her.

Inside the tech room, Chloe pulls up the voice track and hears Tony ask Saunders to speak to Michelle. Chloe picks up the phone to notify someone but the line is dead. Tony has locked down the tech room systems. Chloe is trapped inside.

Tony enters a holding room, knocks out the security guard and takes Jane Saunders.

Kim notices Chloe hasn't refreshed her system. They override the access code to the tech room and find Chloe locked inside. She tells Jack that Saunders is using Michelle to get his daughter out of CTU.

As Tony drives Jane out, Jack locks down the CTU complex. He has less than thirty minutes until the satellite spots him.

09:56

10:55

10:00–11:00

As CTU staff track Tony's car, Jack follows. Tony admits to Jane he has kidnapped her so he can get his wife back from her father.

An SUV swerves into Tony's car and Jack confronts him with a gun. Jack says he knows what Tony is going through but he needs Jane to lure Saunders. Tony is going to a public payphone for instructions.

Jack listens as Tony takes Saunders's phone call. He gives Tony a location but Tony claims the spot is in a CTU satellite area. He refuses to change location and Jack hangs up. Saunders calls back and offers a new meeting spot.

Jack's plan has worked. Chase will now have time to get a team in place at the new location.

As they head to the Sixth Street Bridge, Jack calls Chase to give him a plan of attack. Jack tells Jane that Saunders thinks the country betrayed him even though his job required him to make impossible sacrifices.

10:34 Michelle screams from the holding cell. Saunders's henchman sees she has a bloody nose and is frightened she has the virus. But Michelle has bloodied her own nose and knocks him out with a brick. She grabs his gun and cell phone but it won't work in the underground fortress.

Michelle reaches daylight but is trapped in a dead end. She calls CTU and Kim connects her with Jack. He wants her to be recaptured by Saunders so they have a reason for an exchange. Michelle allows Saunders to find her.

The convoy carrying Michelle arrives at the meeting point. Michelle and Jane pass each other as they walk to opposite sides. Jane hesitates and starts to return to Tony. Saunders appears. The SWAT team and Tony open fire.

Saunders flees to a riverbed toward a waiting helicopter. Jack calls for air support. Marines arrive in F-18 fighter jets and their missiles blow up the helicopter. Jack demands Saunders reveals the location of the unaccounted vials.

10:41 Senator Keeler accuses the President of lying to the police about Alan Milliken's death and shows his proof. Keeler calls for Palmer's resignation once the terrorist threat is resolved. Palmer orders Keeler out of his office and yells at Sherry for sending Keeler to blackmail him. She says Palmer tossed her aside after she performed his dirty work and is willing to go to jail to make her ex-husband pay.

Wayne wonders if they should steal the evidence from Sherry. He secretly meets Bruce Foxton in a parking garage and asks him to retrieve the medicine bottle from Sherry. Wayne says the President knows about the covert operation.

11:10

11:52

11:00-12:00

Saunders admits to Jack that the virus will be released from the eleven missing vials at noon. He will only give their locations if the President guarantees he can flee to North Africa.

11:07 At Jack's request Jane approaches Saunders and begs him to stop the virus. Saunders claims what he is doing will better the world.

Jack and Saunders arrive at the Chandler Plaza Hotel by helicopter and Saunders is unmoved as he is shown body bags full of innocent victims.

Chase brings Jane from a second helicopter and Jack prepares to send her into the infected hotel unless Saunders co-operates. Saunders relents and tells Jack the vials are tagged with GPS codes. He has memorised all eleven locator codes.

With the GPS signals traced, CTU has ten of the eleven vials in their sights. The missing vial is in Los Angeles, its courier is only known to Saunders as Arthur Rabens. Adam is asked to search for aliases of Rabens. With Tony in custody, Brad Hammond has taken over and asks Jack to bring him up to speed.

Hammond tells Tony his act of treason is punishable by the death penalty. The best he can hope for is twenty years in prison. Michelle is stunned to hear Tony let Saunders escape.

11:43 CTU intercepts ten couriers and Chloe puts Jack and Chase onto the trail of Rabens who is in Los Angeles.

The tracking suggests they are directly behind the target but there is no car in front. Jack realises Rabens is in the subway.

Chloe holds back the train as she gets undercover and Hazmat teams in place. As the train arrives at the station, Rabens's vague description is fed to agents over their earwigs.

The GPS tracker shows him leaving the station and Jack narrows it down to four men before pin-pointing someone who has stopped to look at the subway map.

Jack kicks the man down and Chase sweeps his shopping bag with a wand and discovers the transmitter in a pack of cigarettes. The man claims he doesn't smoke. Rabens has slipped the transmitter into the bag.

Jack locks down the station. Everyone who got off the train is still there.

11:44 Palmer asks Sherry to meet him. He plans to distract her whilst Wayne searches for the incriminating prescription bottle at her home.

Wayne takes a call from Julia Milliken, who is about to be arrested for her husband's murder. She knows the President lied to protect Sherry. Julia begs for help.

Wayne and Foxton break into Sherry's house but can't find the prescription bottle.

Palmer offers Sherry a job as a high-level consultant. Sherry wants to be his First Lady again. Surprisingly, Palmer agrees. Sherry is suspicious and says she will help Keeler instead.

Palmer phones Wayne and warns Sherry is on her way back.

Sherry returns, spots Wayne and accuses him of doing the President's dirty work. Foxton appears from behind a wall and knocks Sherry out. The bottle is taped to her back.

Wayne and Foxton are leaving as Julia pulls up. Sherry is regaining consciousness as Julia threatens to shoot her for murdering her husband.

Wayne pleads with Julia to drop the gun. But she puts two shots into Sherry and kills her. She then takes her own life.

12:00-13:00

Hammond takes Tony's statement about working against the agency during the Saunders case. Tony admits to putting Michelle's life ahead of national security.

12:05 Gael's wife, Theresa, arrives and Kim takes her to Gael's workstation to pick up his personal belongings. Theresa notices a computer monitor showing a profile of Saunders, and realises this is the terrorist responsible for her husband's death.

A handcuffed Saunders is led to the Field Ops office to examine screen shots from the subway station in a bid to identify Rabens. Before he can do anything, Saunders is shot by Theresa with a gun from Gael's desk.

12:19 As Jack has every train passenger thoroughly searched, Chase reveals he is transferring out of Field Ops so he can look after both Kim and his baby. Jack offers his support.

Jack notices a man has disappeared and radios Chase. Two LAPD officers are down as he and Chase leave the underground station. Another man lies stabbed on the street, killed in a carjacking.

Jack takes the dead man's license and gets Michelle to look up his car registration as he and Chase get in their SUV. Michelle tells Hammond they are understaffed and need Tony's help. Hammond reluctantly agrees.

By scanning traffic cameras, Chloe and Adam find the car carrying Rabens. Two CTU cars block the vehicle but Rabens runs into a school.

Chase enters an empty science lab and Rabens slashes his gun arm. The device holding the virus falls out of a bag. Chase clamps the device to his arm. Rabens activates the release of the virus. Jack arrives and kills Rabens.

12:41

12:46

12:41 The clamp cannot be unlocked. Jack is put onto a team who have disarmed the other devices and an agent leads him through dismantling the device. There is less than four minutes and the green wire Jack needs to cut is not there!

Chase spots an axe in the fire extinguisher box and Jack reluctantly chops off Chase's arm and throws it inside a fridge in the teachers' lounge. The device releases the virus into the sealed refrigerator.

12:53 Wayne informs his brother that Julia killed Sherry and then turned the gun on herself. The President dismisses him.

Palmer phones Jack in hospital to personally thank him for all he has done for the country and apologises for making him kill Chappelle. The President reveals he is not seeking re-election.

Kim hugs her father. Chase is in surgery and the doctors are optimistic about his recovery. As Jack leaves the hospital he answers the call to help interrogate Saunders's couriers. He wipes away his tears and heads back to work.

12:39

JACK'S ARMOURY

Why you shouldn't mess with Jack...

HECKLER AND KOCH USP COMPACT

It's not the biggest handgun in the world but the USP Compact packs a big 9mm punch.

Smaller and lighter than the large frame USP, this gun can easily be hidden under clothing and is pretty easy to shoot with one hand.

To make it even more attractive this gun can fire off in excess of 20,000 rounds during its lifetime..

RUGER MINI 14

American-made, this semi automatic is also favoured by police and military. One version even has a bayonet lug and folding stock for paratrooper use.

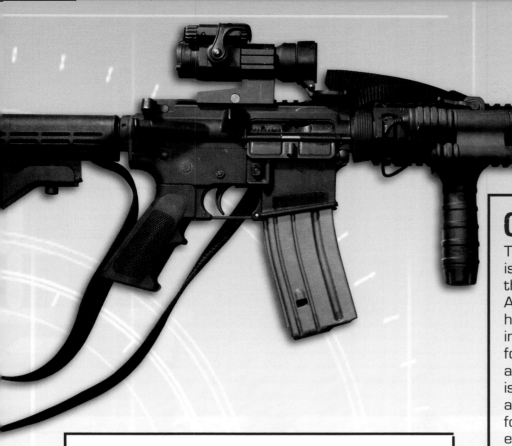

COLT M4 CARBINE

The M4A1 Carbine assault rifle is a very popular weapon with the military and is being used in Afghanistan and Iraq. Jack's version has had several upgrades that include a laser sight, and a vertical foregrip. It can also be used as a semi-automatic. This weapon is light, can be used with speed and is the first-line weapon of choice for many Special Forces. It can even be adapted to cater for different sized soldiers!.

HECKLER AND KOCH MP5

The MP5 is one of the most used and most famous sub machine guns in the world, so no surprise to find them used by Jack! They can fire hundreds of rounds per minute. There are other HK's in Jack's armoury, including the USP compact, which is a smaller, lighter handgun than his SIG, but which can fire similar cartridges.

German-made, this weapon has stood the test of time, the original version having surface in 1966. Even when the updated UMP was developed H & K kept on making the MP5.

SIG P228

When it comes to firepower, there are very few people who could match Jack Bauer's armoury!The CTU's star man is a walking arsenal of top guns and wicked knives with which to take on and defeat his opponents.

The SIG P228, 9mm with stainless steel slides. This handgun is among the most reliable around. Although it can carry up to 14 rounds in a chamber, law enforcement chiefs prefer officers to carry 10 to 12 rounds to make the guns more efficient and guard against jamming.

DAY THREE: QUIZ

Test your knowledge of 24 with this quiz. Is your memory for detail as sharp as Jack Bauer's? Answers are on page 126.

01: Which nationality were the scientists who engineered the deadly virus?

(A) Russian (B) Ukrainian (C) Armenian

02: What is the name of the deadly virus?

(A) Cordilla (B) Campolla (C) Cranilla

04: What is the name of the hotel where the virus is released?

(A) Chandler Plaza Hotel

(B) Wilshire Plaza Hotel

(C) Los Angeles Plaza Hotel

03: Jack goes undercover within the Salazar drug cartel, but in which country?

(A) Argentina

(B) Columbia

(C) Mexico

05: Who killed Stephen Saunders?

(A) Jack Bauer

(B) Gael Ortega

(C) Theresa Ortega

06: Stephen Saunders' daughter, Jane, goes to college in California, but in which city?

(A) San Diego

(B) Santa Barbara

(C) San Francisco

07: Who planted the virus at the hotel?

(A) Michael Amador

(B) Marcus Alvers

(C) Arthur Rabens

09: How did President Palmer meet Anne Packard?

(A) She was his Doctor

(B) She was his PA

(C) She was his political advisor

08: How was Michael Amador killed?

(A) Shot

(B) Killed by virus

(C) Bomb

10: What is the name of Chase's daughter?

(A) Andrea

(B) Angela

(C) Amelia

11: What is the phrase Stephen Saunders demands President Palmer uses in his press conference?

(A) "The sky is falling"

(B) "The world is changing"

(C) "American safety is our top priority"

12: What is Tony Almeida arrested for?

(A) Murder

(B) Kidnapping

(C) Treason

THE STORY SO FAR...
Your quick guide to what has happened in every season of 24

DAY ONE

A group of mercenaries kidnap Jack Bauer's wife and daughter and refuse to release them until he kills Presidential candidate David Palmer. The Drazen brothers are behind the kidnap as they try to rescue their father Victor who has been secretly imprisoned by the government. Jack thought he had killed Victor during an operation in Kosovo two years earlier. Nina Myers is revealed at a mole inside CTU. She kills Jack's wife Teri but is exiled from America, her pardon for helping to track down the Drazens.

DAY TWO

Set one year after the end of Day One, Palmer is now President and Jack Bauer has to be re-commissioned as an agent to take on terrorists who threaten to explode a nuclear bomb in Los Angeles. The bomb is discovered and flown into the desert on a suicide mission started by Jack but finished by radiation victim George Mason. Three Middle East countries are linked to the bomb in a fake recording. Jack has to prove the recording is false to help stop the outbreak of a possible World War – and save the President from being deposed. Palmer collapses at the end of the day having being infected by a biological weapon.

DAY THREE

Three years after Palmer was infected the President remains in power but is still an unwell man. His problems are added to when terrorists threaten to release a virus on Los Angeles unless drug baron Ramon Salazar is released from prison. Jack has to go deep undercover to track down the virus, the buyers, and discover the real person behind the threat. Jack is forced to kill a colleague to save LA and discovers that former intelligence officer Stephen Saunders is to blame for the crisis. Palmer does not stand for re-election.

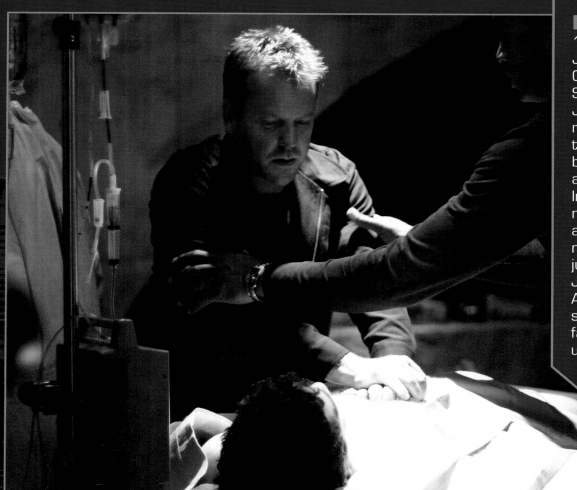

DAY FOUR

15 months later, Jack has been fired by CTU and works for Secretary of Defense James Heller. But Jack returns to CTU to take on terrorist Habib Marwan and battle a series of attacks against the United States. Internet chaos, nuclear plant meltdowns, the bombing of a commuter train and a massive blackout in LA are just some of the disasters Jack has to confront. A missile heading for LA is shot down – but Jack has to fake his own death and go underground when the new President, Logan, issues orders for his death.

DAY FIVE

A further 18 months on, Jack Bauer is a labourer at an oil refinery in California. It is the day President Logan is due to sign an anti-terrorist agreement with Russia at his Californian retreat. Jack is framed for the murders of former President Palmer and ex-colleague Michelle Dessler but instead of facing trial has to take on terrorists who have stolen nerve gas and taken 40 people hostage. He discovers Logan is not all he appears and has to help bring him down. As the day ends, Jack is on board a ship to Shanghai after the Chinese government have discovered he is still alive. They want him for the death of their country's consul 18 months earlier.

DAY SIX

President Wayne Palmer – the late David's brother – negotiates Jack's release from China and hands him over to Abu Fayed in return for the location of the man behind suicide bombings all over the US. But Jack discovers Fayed is really the man behind the attacks and plans nuclear strikes. He escapes and joins forces with Assad, the man accused of setting up the suicide bombers, but who is actually trying to prevent the attacks. A bomb explodes killing an initial 12,000 people, Palmer dies as a result of an attack and Jack has to deal with Russian and Chinese threats and interference as he attempts to save his country.

DAY SEVEN

Three years and ten months later, Jack is in Africa having disappeared following his battles of Day Six. It's inauguration day for President Allison Taylor. The CTU has been disbanded. Jack returns to face a Senate hearing but is enlisted to track down a threat to the nation's computers. Two planes collide over the White House killing hundreds of passengers and Jack sides with former colleague Tony Almeida to take on conspirators and retrieve vital electronic equipment. But his return to action sees him infected by a bio weapon and daughter Kim has to undergo a stem cell procedure to save her father's life.

...AND DAY EIGHT!

Jack is back! It's just seven weeks after Day Seven. CTU returns. New York is the setting. It's the city that never sleeps. And you'd better be wide-awake to follow Jack's latest adventures!

ANSWERS

DAY ONE: QUIZ

01 What was the name of Jack Bauer's military mission in Kosovo?

(B) Operation Nightfall

02 What nationality was Victor Drazen?

(A) Serbian

03 What is the name of Kim's friend, who was kidnapped with her?

(B) Janet York

04 Who did Teri Bauer have an affair with?

(A) Dr Phil Parslow

05 What is the name given to the US political primaries that take place on the same day, usually in early March?

(C) Super Tuesday

06 Who did Kevin Carroll pretend to be in order to help Ira Gaines kidnap Teri Bauer?

(A) Alan York

07 What kind of scandal was David Palmer's son, Keith, involved in?

(C) Murder

08 How many primaries did David Palmer win?

(B) 11

09 What is the name of David Palmer's daughter?

(C) Nicole

10 Prior to his presidency, where did David Palmer serve as Congressman and Senator?

(A) Maryland

11 What is Jack Bauer's masters degree in?

(B) Criminology and Law

12 Who was hired by the Drazens to assassinate Senator David Palmer?

(B) Ira Gaines

DAY TWO: QUIZ

01 How is CTU's Special Agent in Charge, George Mason, injured in the field?

(C) Poisoned

02 What is the name of the child that Kim cares for?

(B) Megan

03 Who was granted a full presidential pardon?

(A) Nina Myers

04 Who is the leader of Coral Snake?

(B) Jonathan Wallace

05 How are members of Coral Snake identified?

(B) Snake tattoo

06 Where does the first scene of the season take place?

(B) Seoul, South Korea

07 Which medical problem does Jack develop after being held by terrorists?

(A) Heart condition

08 Where was the fake recording from?

(C) Cyprus

09 What nationality was Max, the arms dealer?

(B) German

10 Which airfield did the plane carrying the bomb take off from?

(B) Norton

11 How did Alex Hewitt die?

(A) Blood loss

12 What is the name of the Vice-President who invoked the 25th amendment?

(C) Jim Prescott

DAY THREE: QUIZ

01 Which nationality were the scientists who engineered the deadly virus?

(B) Ukrainian

02 What is the name of the deadly virus?

(A) Cordilla

03 Jack goes undercover within the Salazar drug cartel, but in which country?

(C) Mexico

04 What is the name of the hotel where the virus is released?

(A) Chandler Plaza Hotel

05 Who killed Stephen Saunders?

(C) Theresa Ortega

06 Stephen Saunders' daughter, Jane, goes to college in California, but in which city?

(B) Santa Barbara

07 Who planted the virus at the hotel?

(B) Marcus Alvers

08 How was Michael Amador killed?

(C) Bomb

09 How did President Palmer meet Anne Packard?

(A) She was his doctor

10 What is the name of Chase's daughter?

(B) Angela

11 What is the phrase Stephen Saunders demands President Palmer uses in his press conference?

(A) "The sky is falling"

12 What is Tony Almeida arrested for?

(C) Treason